BREAKTHROUGH

SOLD SEPARATELY

Get Out of the Boat of Mediocrity
and Walk On Water

BRANDI HARVEY

Breakthrough Sold Separately
Get Out of the Boat of Mediocrity and Walk On Water

ISBN 978-1-7340552-0-7

Library of Congress Control Number: 2019915246

Published by:
BEYOND HER
6425 Powers Ferry Road, NW
Suite 198
Atlanta, GA 30339

*To my mother Marcia. Thank you for teaching
me to serve the needs of God's people. The
world has finally become my classroom.*

*To my father Steve. Thank you for teaching me how
to fly. The push propelled me into my destiny.*

Through devotion, blessed are the children.

CONTENTS

YOUR GREATNESS IS
WAITING ON YOU

I WAS ABOUT TO BE FIRED from my job as the executive director of the Steve and Marjorie Harvey Foundation. However, when I boarded the plane from Atlanta to Los Angeles, where I would meet with my dad to discuss my role in his foundation, a calmness and an ease settled in my spirit. The few months of therapy I'd committed to so far seemed to be working. I kept telling myself, "Brandi, just accept the things you can't change."

With a two-day turnaround, I knew I had to make the most of my time. Since he had avoided me for months, I was heading to L.A. to force my dad's hand. I needed him to see me. I needed him to offer me some guidance and show me the right direction. Known to run from any form of conflict with his children, I knew my dad would try his best to escape any tough conversation he believed might come his way. And I was right. When I arrived, we exchanged pleasantries and small talk, but my dad mostly avoided me in the house. He busied himself with meetings and work. He didn't say a word about it, but in my heart, I knew this would be my final bow as the leader of his organization.

Weeks earlier, he had sent me a text message saying he was thinking of going in a different direction with the foundation, and I'd responded, "I figured as much." I was well aware that I hadn't been performing at my highest level, and we could only go on so long that way. Even though I'd texted him several times since then, he never answered. When I expressed my frustration to a co-worker, she told me, "Every daughter needs her father's blessing," and she advised me to go to him and ask for his guidance. I texted my dad and told him, "I don't need a lot of your time. I just need your blessing as your daughter." He'd responded that I should come out to L.A. so we could talk, but once I got there, he seemed to want to do everything but talk with me about what was going on between us.

Sitting by the pool at my dad's house, I knew things would change that day, but I had no idea how it would happen. It didn't take long to find out. When I picked up my phone to check my email, there it was in plain black and white: "We would like to welcome the new executive director of the Steve and Marjorie Harvey Foundation." My heart dropped, and a lump formed in my throat. Someone else had been hired to do what had, until that moment, been my job. I checked the details of the message and saw with clear eyes that the email had gone company-wide.

My sister, Karli, and my brother Broderick were with me, and they both saw the email when I did. Their eyes widened in disbelief, and my sister asked, "Are you reading what I'm reading?" Almost left without words, I answered, "Yep." Just like the character Craig, played by Ice Cube in the movie *Friday*, I had been fired on my day off. I wasn't angry because, like most people who get fired, I'd known it was coming long before it happened. I just didn't know what I would do next. In my dad's mind the "different direction" text message he'd sent me weeks earlier had probably sufficed as notice that I was being let go, but to me, it had been the beginning of the conversation, not the end.

That evening, my dad and I finally talked. We cleared the air, which had grown thick with tension. Years of failing to clearly communicate with each other had filled the hazy space between us with assumptions and misgivings about one another. He expressed his need to make changes at the foundation and explained that he believed my dismissal would release me to soar to higher heights. I explained to him that I felt like I could easily be mad about how the whole thing had gone down, but I also knew it was time. I was given a severance package, and my dad told me he'd always be there for me whenever I needed him. I really needed him to tell me what I was good at, reassure me about my talents and abilities, and give me the best option for this next chapter of my life. Instead, he told me, "Sometimes you don't jump, Brandi. Sometimes you're pushed."

It was a difficult conversation, but it was also the first time we talked to each other as two adults, and I was grateful for that. I didn't dive into the messy part of the way things had gone. Instead, I focused on the fact that my dad finally respected me as an adult. I walked away from the conversation unsure of the future, but content in knowing things had worked out as they should have. I'd created and accomplished great things in my work at the foundation, but that time had come to its natural end.

I now know that, on that late summer day, I wasn't fired. As my friend Allyson told me, I was released into my destiny. On that day, I got out of the boat of mediocrity and began my journey of walking on water. To say I was scared would be an understatement: I was terrified. I had just turned thirty-five years old three days prior to losing my job, and I felt like time was closing in on me. I felt like I needed to make something happen for myself, but I committed to consistent therapy appointments going forward, and doing that work reminded me I was right on schedule.

Eventually, I got the breakthrough I was looking for in my life, but it took time, it took energy, and it took a whole lot of effort. It was on the other side of all the years that I cried, drank myself to sleep, and tried to numb the pain with sex. Getting out of the boat of mediocrity was hard. I was weighed down by my insecurities and tied to my victim story, but once I finally let them go, I also untied myself from flawed relationships that no longer served me, the need to please people before pleasing God, and the shame I'd felt for failing.

In the following weeks and months, I realized I was not alone. The moment I accepted the divine invitation to live on purpose, God met me on the water of my destiny. All that time, I'd thought I was struggling by myself, and there, within me, was my love, my grace, my Savior. The moment I got out of the boat of mediocrity, my faith was put to the test. Over the last two years, that test has shown me that my power was within me all along. Getting fired on August 23, 2017, and sending this book to the publisher two years later, to the date, is nothing but God.

Jesus performed miracles and changed the world, and what Jesus did, we can all do. There is a Christ—an anointed one chosen by God for a special purpose—within you that must be fulfilled. In no way is this meant to pull Jesus down to my level or the level of the average person. Instead, recognizing the Christ within us is a call to raise our ways of thinking and living to his level. You have limitless potential within you. To create and bring to life all that you wish to see in this lifetime and the next. The real sin is to not discover your own Christ-like power and potential. To not tap into the divine while here on the planet may be the biggest transgression of all.

Breakthrough Sold Separately is an invitation for you to go beyond the life you've lived so far and begin your journey within. Your greatness is waiting on you to answer the call to tap into your divinity, live to your highest potential, and become the best version of you. This book is my gift to you. Let it serve as your freedom papers and your license to break every chain that has kept you stuck in the boat of mediocrity. If you're ready to journey deeper and heal your life, turn the page. This is your time to walk on water. You won't win unless you begin.

Love and Grace,
BH

1

LOSE TO WIN

I F YOU WANT TO BECOME the best, you work with the best to get you there. When I decided I wanted to be a fitness competitor in 2007, I talked with eight-time Mr. Olympia Lee Haney and asked him to train me. Instead, Lee referred me to a husband-and-wife team. When I walked in for my consultation with Roc and Gina, their gym was so new it still had papers on the floor to mark where the equipment would go. The gym might not have been ready, but I was. At that time, I taught spin classes, I worked out every day, and I thought I was in good shape. I told Roc, "I want to compete in December." It was already October, but I really believed I could snap into competition shape over the next three months. At the latest, I thought, I'd be competing by the time the new year rolled around.

Roc stared at me for a moment before he responded, "How about you just start the program? Then we'll decide when you'll be ready to get on the stage." I agreed, but I kept that December goal in mind.

At twenty-four years old, I didn't consider myself a particularly self-disciplined person, so I wanted someone who would help me develop that trait. I wanted someone who would push me, and I got exactly that. In my first training session with Roc, he told me to lunge down the floor and back. "Oh, I don't do lunges," I said, fully expecting he would give me a different exercise to do. My previous trainer had always been easily swayed by my personal preferences. If I didn't feel like doing lunges, she didn't try to force me to do them. If I felt like sitting on the bench and talking, she and I would sit and chat. Roc had a different response to my refusal: "If you don't get them weights in your hands and do them f-cking lunges . . . " I did what he said.

The three months I'd planned to spend training for my first fitness competition came and went. It took me nine months to be ready to get onstage and stand next to the other women who had sacrificed to cut and mold their physiques to what most people would consider an impossible standard. In that time, I discovered I had to change some things to have a chance of accomplishing my goal. There was no place for mediocrity on my road to competing. I had to meal prep, stick to the diet, follow a specific training schedule, and bring a new focus and intention to my workouts. I had to lift heavy and do a crazy number of reps. And whether I liked them or not, I had to do those lunges.

I didn't win my first and only fitness competition. I had done the work, and I went in confident I would take home the big trophy. So when they called my number for second place, I just stood there. I didn't step forward because there was no way I had come in any place but first. They had to call my number again before I accepted that I had lost. Backstage, my mother and sister told me they felt like I'd been robbed of the title. I agreed, and I was pissed. *Nobody remembers who won the silver medal*, I thought.

After I calmed down and had time to reflect on my experience, I realized I had, in fact, won. I'd won because I got up on that stage and did what I'd committed to do. I'd won because I trained like a beast, stuck to a schedule, and measured out six ounces of chicken and half a cup of broccoli while everyone else at the table ate macaroni and cheese. I'd won because I zeroed in on my goal with total focus, locked and loaded. I'd been willing to lose the distractions in order to win. In the end, I discovered I didn't need anyone to teach me discipline. I had that self-discipline inside of me. I just needed to tap into it and apply it.

This journey you're on is so much more than one moment on a stage. This is your life. To go to the next level, you'll have to leave somethings behind, including some of your beliefs. That doesn't mean you turn your back on your family or all the things that have made you wonderfully, colorfully human. Losing some things means making room for God's goodness in your life. Losing doesn't always equal defeat; sometimes it's the setup for your triumphant victory. To win, you have to lose the stories you keep telling yourself. Those stories usually begin and end with excuses, and they keep you stuck at the intersection of stagnant and complacent. To get next-level blessings, you have to lose the blessing-blockers in your life.

The work I'm inviting you to do requires you to be willing to lose in order to win.

My experience as a fitness competitor is emblematic of the journey on which you're about to embark. Just like I pushed my body beyond what had, up until that time, been its limits, this journey will push you beyond your limits. Beyond is where your truth and your power lie. When you work out, you have to push your muscles beyond their limits because that's when the growth occurs. I'm inviting you to push your life beyond its limits so you can grow your consciousness, your capacity for love, and your self-awareness. I'm cheering you on to push yourself to reach a new level of health and wholeness in your body, mind, and spirit and create a richer, fuller life for yourself. It's all connected, and growth in one area will position you for growth in every area. But you will have to push yourself in new ways. You'll have to demand more of yourself.

As you move, the Divine will move with you so that your efforts are multiplied. As you do this work, you will see your life open up. This transformation starts with the internal shifts that will make it all possible. You'll need to:

+ Make the choice to do this work.
+ Be willing to change.
+ Question everything.
+ Submit to foundational principles.
+ Tell the truth.
+ Be unwilling to settle.

MAKE THE CHOICE TO DO THIS WORK

When Roc pushed me to do the exercises I'd always hated and to lift heavier than I ever had before, I had a choice. I could choose to do the work, or I could quit. If I was going to do it though, I had to go all in. Doing it halfway was never going to serve me. Doing the exercises and cheating on the meal plan wasn't going to produce the results I wanted. Eating perfectly but skipping workouts would have been a waste of my time. I had to follow the plan.

The work you're doing here is a little different from what I was doing in the gym. It's infinitely more important. This is your life we're dealing with here. This is personal and individualized work, and you'll have to customize it to create what you want. You'll follow a plan, but it won't look like the next person's plan. It won't necessarily look like mine either. You don't need to take on my personal beliefs or live the way I do. However, if you want real results, you will have to deal with yourself on a physical, mental, spiritual, and emotional level. You don't have to do it all at once. You don't have to do it all my way. But you have to do it all.

This is heart work, and heart work is hard work. Don't quit when you start to feel the stress of it. Don't give up because you don't see immediate results, or when your friends start to question why you don't tolerate the same foolishness anymore. Make a commitment to yourself to see it through, in ways big and small, every day.

BE WILLING TO CHANGE

Look at pictures of me from my sister's wedding in 2015 and compare them to pictures of me in 2016. I'm clearly bigger in the later photos. In the weeks before Karli's wedding, I joined her in cutting our meals down to green juice and almonds, and we hit the gym hard. We were serious about looking our best for her big day. However, in the following months, like most people who lose weight for a specific event, I gained back every pound I'd lost. Sure, I looked great in the wedding pictures, but it was a temporary change. After all of that effort, I went right back to my old habits.

Change is not going to come from doing the same things you did last year, last month, or yesterday. Change isn't going to come from outside of you. In order to get something different, you will have to do things differently. You'll have to stop saying, "That's just who I am," and be willing to become someone new. You'll have to step out of your comfort zone and endure some discomfort. Even when you don't see immediate results, you will have to persist. When it hurts—and sometimes it will—remember your commitment. Choose to change so you can be the best version of yourself.

Superficial changes won't get you the results you want. You have to dig up the roots. It's not enough to recognize that you overeat, for example, and decide to stop. If you don't understand why you make bad food choices in the first place, you'll end up back in the same place again, struggling to get into your Spanx and complaining about how you don't have time to go to the gym. If you don't get to the reasons why you choose unavailable men, or why you put up with being cheated on, or why you keep going to a job you hate, or why you continue to put yourself last in your life in innumerable ways, you will continue to get everything you say you don't want. Dig deep and prepare to change at the deepest levels of who you are.

QUESTION EVERYTHING

You cannot change your life until you're willing to question everything you believe. This is hardest to do when you come from a background that discourages you from talking back to authority or questioning what's handed down from on high. When the people closest to you cling to their beliefs, they often expect you to do the same. This can be especially difficult when those are the people you call family, which comes with its own unique set of challenges. However, it's possible to still love and respect those people closest to you and evolve in ways they don't understand. In recent years, I've experienced that kind of transformation in my life.

In 2017, I travelled to the Art of Living Center, in the Blue Ridge Mountains, for a five-day silent meditation retreat. For our final activity on the last day, we were instructed to sit across from another person in the group as we were guided through a meditation on divinity. Each of us locked eyes with the person across from us, peering into their soul. Each of us was looking at the Divine.

Repeatedly, we were asked, "If God showed up in this form, could you love, could you accept the Creator in this form, just as they are? Could you accept yourself as divine?" I was deeply moved by the beauty and honesty of that moment. Nipun was the second person out of three who came to sit in front of my own divine spirit. He came with tears in his eyes, and when I reached out and held his hands, he cried more. I too began to cry. Not because I was sad, but because I understood that I was, in fact, looking at God. The Divine.

If God showed up as male or female, Black, White, Indian, or Asian—no matter the race, color, or sexual orientation—could I love? Could I trust? Could I accept? In that moment, I knew I could. I finally let go of all the judgments and preconceived notions about people that I'd carried all my life. I was the Divine, and God was staring right back at me. How beautiful that God could be so infinite and omnipotent and morph into all forms. God as male and female, as every race, color, creed, or religious belief. God was there on that mountain with me, a part of me. How small I would be if I shortchanged the beauty and vastness of the divine presence of God by failing to see that presence in everyone around me. We all have divinity within us. The true blessing is when we uncover it in ourselves and the moment we open our eyes to see God all around us.

That time on the mountain humbled me. I joined an allegiance of souls around the world who took the journey inward. I was humbled by God's grace and the knowledge that it was just the beginning of my journey. Life became bigger and more fulfilling. I am grateful for the mountains and the opportunity to sit where heaven meets earth and spend time in communion with God's divine beauty.

My views on the divinity within all of us contradict some of the fundamental tenets with which I was raised. My family and many of my friends hold sacred those beliefs. While I respect and honor their right to choose what they believe, I had to discover the truth for myself. I couldn't be held back by the notion that we're never to question authority, never to question our parents, never to question the church. It is the truth that sets us free.

You don't have to think the way your tribe thinks about everything in your life. You may find that some of what has been passed down in your family for generations doesn't work for you. In that case, bless and release it. You'll likely get some negative reactions, but look at it this way: If the beliefs in which you've placed your total faith cannot stand up to questioning, you're building your life on a shaky foundation. Questioning what you've always thought to be true will either reinforce your beliefs, giving you a fuller, richer understanding of them, or it will open you to new beliefs that may serve you better.

SUBMIT TO FOUNDATIONAL PRINCIPLES

Eventually, if you practice them consistently, the beliefs you decide to hold on to and the new ones you add will become foundational principles for the way you live. Those foundational principles, within which you choose to always operate, will actually make it easier for you to take on the new habits you'll need to become this higher version of yourself. Because I don't eat fast food, for example, I don't have to make a decision about whether or not I should just hit the drive-thru when I don't feel like making a meal. I'm committed to going to therapy every week, so I don't have to debate with myself on Wednesday mornings. Healthy plant-based eating and therapy are foundational principles to which I submit. Those decisions are made in advance, so I don't have to keep making them over and over, day after day, week after week.

I'll offer you the principles that work for me, but only you can decide which will be the foundational principles for your life. The important thing is to commit to the principles you choose to live under. Over time, when you consistently honor them, they'll become ingrained in the way you live. They will become habits you no longer have to struggle to practice. They will become your lifestyle. You will have mastered one level and be ready to move on to the next.

TELL THE TRUTH

I was hanging out with a guy friend one day when he told me something that completely surprised me. "B, I just want my momma to love me," he said. I wasn't surprised by the fact that he still had a deep need to feel loved and accepted by his mother. What amazed me was how clearly he saw the truth about himself and his openness in sharing it with me. I was grateful that he trusted me enough and thought enough of our relationship to choose me as his confidante. That he could stand in that truth said a lot about his own self-awareness and honesty.

It's a lot easier to know what principles to live your life by when you're honest with yourself about your needs, wants, shortcomings, and strengths. Moments of true transparency and vulnerability can seem rare in our busy lives, but when they happen, they leave an impression. They make a difference. Telling the truth about yourself, especially to yourself, will get you where you want to be a lot faster. This is a form of accountability, the greatest act of self-love.

When you hire a trainer or work with a life coach, that person gives you a level of external accountability, but the real accountability is answering to yourself for the decisions you make and taking responsibility for your intentions, your choices, and your results. This requires learning to live in the fullness of who you are without shame and without need for approval. Who are you willing to be when no one else is looking? Holding yourself accountable requires you to examine your life with complete honesty. It requires you to keep your promises and commitments to yourself with the same level of integrity you apply to keeping your word to other people.

In some areas of my life, like my relationship with my father, taking ownership took me years to do. For the longest time, I was angry with my dad for abandoning me. I felt rejected and neglected, and I made my life choices fueled by those feelings and emotions. I chose to operate out of that pain. But I was hurting our relationship by failing to recognize my dad as a person with his own emotions. I didn't even consider that he had a side in the discussion. It was just about me. I was stuck in my story and feeding on the drama of it. I was so busy pointing a finger at him that I couldn't see I hadn't been the best daughter to him either. While he could have been a more physically and emotionally present father for much of my life, I also bore some responsibility for the state of our relationship. Holding myself accountable didn't negate anything that had happened between us, but I had to own the fact that I was no longer a powerless little girl. I was a grown woman, responsible for my power and how I chose to use it.

Getting honest with yourself also requires you to look under the labels other people have given you and the roles you play. If you've been cast as the smart girl, the fast girl, the funny girl, the drama queen, the pretty girl, the ugly girl, or the martyr, know that's not who you are. It's just a role you've played. Often the adults who pass out these labels do so out of ignorance, out of a desire to protect children from judgment, to toughen them up, or to set a standard for them to meet. Whatever the intention, the results are the same— women who spend a lifetime trying to live up to or run away from the box they were put in as little girls. You are much more than the label you've worn, and you can choose today to shed the character you've played and step into being you. If you don't know exactly who that is yet, don't worry. At the heart of this journey is discovering you. You get to honor your truth and choose your story.

In the past, my self-image included living a luxurious life-style for the sake of impressing other people. For a long time, I bought into the images of material luxury and a life of leisure as the definitions of success. The constant money porn on Instagram, people posting images of their latest acquisitions— from cars to houses and designer bags and shoes—seemed like the way to happiness. I pursued those things with some success, but I could never fill the void in my life.

While I do enjoy luxury, I didn't understand how much of that posing was a cover for low self-esteem. The houses, the cars, the bags, the shoes, the invitations—the women I sought to emulate seem to have it all, and I was chasing what I thought they had. I wanted to be validated in that circle of women, but so much of what I saw was an illusion. Once I looked closely at it, I realized my eyes had been playing tricks on me. In so many cases, what looked like success was the same kind of desperate need for external validation that I was experiencing.

To move beyond the need for other people to validate my worth, I had to get quiet and search within myself. I had to accept that what looked like luxury was really a trap when there was nothing joyful, wonderful, or magical about it. I had to get honest with myself and hold myself accountable. The women I wanted to be like weren't at fault. Just like I had, they were looking outside of themselves to find happiness. They'd designed their lives based on what they believed would stop the pain, but I'd proven in my own life that material things can't fix what's wrong. Finally, I decided I could no longer settle for an outward appearance of success. Contrary to popular belief, material success is much easier to come by than peace of mind, but peace of mind is so much more valuable. Once I recognized that truth, it was my responsibility to deal with it in my own life and model a better way.

BE UNWILLING TO SETTLE

It's easy to see when someone else is settling for less than she deserves. It can be much harder to see it in yourself. In fact, if you had asked me a few years ago, I would've told you that, no, I don't settle. I would've said my standards were high, but that was only partially true. I did set the bar high in some areas of my life, but in other areas, I was in complete denial about how little I was willing to demand of myself and the people around me. In truth, I was doing what I'd been programmed to do. I was settling for less.

That truth was driven home for me in a conversation during Karli's bachelorette weekend. Twelve of us, including friends from childhood, friends from college, and friends we'd made in our young adulthood, went away together. We all gathered to reminisce, have a good time, and help my twin say goodbye to single life. At brunch that weekend, the conversation ran the gamut of the usual news and gossip. However, this was an assembly of smart, accomplished, ambitious women. Eventually, talk turned to social issues, our personal and professional goals, and why some people stay stuck in their lives while others seem to progress regardless of what challenges they face.

"People are just programmed for less," our friend Arielle said. She tossed out this statement as if it were common knowledge, but it stuck with me, echoing in my thoughts in the following weeks and months. She had so succinctly summed up a painful truth, one I'd long recognized but had never articulated so clearly. People are programmed for less.

Arielle meant that people, especially women, and perhaps black women most of all, are programmed to think less of ourselves. We're programmed by social media and advertisements, television and the movies, school, the larger culture, and sometimes even our own families to believe we deserve less. A steady stream of words and imagery sends the message that you are not enough. You need plastic surgery, bigger breasts, a smaller waist, a higher butt, a nicer car, a more expensive bag, or a man at your side to meet the standard. Nothing about you, it would seem, is good enough as is.

We unconsciously take on the belief that we're less than enough and deserve less than others have, and so we aspire for less in our lives. From an early age, we're programmed to operate in lack. We say we want health, and love, and success in its many forms, but we don't believe we deserve any of it. Not deserving it becomes a victim story that convinces us to settle, but it doesn't have to be that way. The Creator wants us to prosper and live in an abundance of all things good and loving. Be unwilling to settle in any area of your life from now on. Reprogram yourself for more. Shake off victimhood and demand more of yourself, of the people around you, and of life. You may not feel worthy or deserving yet, but if you do the work, you will.

LOSE THE EXCUSES

To have more of the life you desire and stop settling for the leftovers, you're going to have to lose the excuses. Yes, racism, sexism, and classism exist as very real challenges, but they're not our greatest obstacles. Unfortunately, we are our greatest obstacles. We find every reason not to put ourselves first. We don't invest the time to read or to think our way into greatness because we've been taught to look outside ourselves for answers and to settle for what we're told we can have. However, while people and culture have influenced us, good or bad, we are responsible for our lives and the results we get. We choose our routines, rituals, and daily practices, and they either serve us or they harm us. They either bring us closer to who we're destined to be, or they leave us stuck.

It's easy to blame big business, the government, or your bad boss. It's easy to blame your parents for what they did or didn't do in raising you. It's easy to sit around complaining and bonding with your friends over what's wrong in your lives. *Who has the worst relationship? Who has the most debt? Who's on the most medication? Who's carrying the heaviest burden?* Too often, women show up in our circles and try to outdo each other's tragedies. So many of us play the martyr and play it well, but when you become the victim of your own story, you rob yourself of agency. Sometimes, your lack of progress isn't because you're unmotivated and unwilling to fly, it's because you don't even realize you have the potential to get off the ground. But you do, and if you lose the excuses, you will be able to soar.

> Too often, women show up in our circles and try to outdo each other's tragedies.

Some people in your life will be inspired by your change and do their best to fly beside you, but others you'll have to leave behind. They'll try to grab you by the sleeve and hold you back, but if you want to get to the next level, you'll have to shake them off and keep moving forward. At the same time, your transformation will cause other people to turn away of their own accord. They'll take your desire to change as a criticism of their own unwillingness to evolve, and you won't be able to chase them down and pull them along with you. Let them go.

Questioning your old habits, relationships, and choices, and examining whether or not they serve you at the highest level can be scary. Getting honest and holding yourself accountable can be emotionally exhausting. Dropping your crutches when you've never walked without them can be terrifying, but it's the only way. As you enter this process, your circles may get smaller before they get bigger. The things that used to excite you may lose their appeal. Like any new convert, as you feel the awakening of your consciousness, you'll want to spread your gospel and show other people how they can save themselves, but that's not your job—not yet. For now, your job is to work on you and let your light shine so brightly that the people around you can't help but desire a little of what you have. Set an intention for this evolutionary journey you're embarking on. Choose to do the work. Suit up and prepare to become the hero of your own story.

Affirmation

I HAVE THE DIVINE
RIGHT TO HAVE ALL
I DREAM OF HAVING.

2 TAKE OFF THE MASK

I N 1976, THE HIT SITCOM *Good Times* shocked
fans with the death of one its main characters. At the
end of the first episode of the season, Florida Evans is
opening celebratory cards and letters when she's handed a
telegram in the midst of the family's going-away party. The
family is elated to finally have a chance to escape the ghetto
they've lived in for decades, and Florida expects to read a sexy
love note from her husband, who has gone ahead of the family
to Mississippi to take advantage of a new career opportunity.

Surrounded by friends and family, Florida reads aloud,
her voice filled with excitement and joy, "Dear Mrs. Evans,
that's me, we regret to inform you that your husband, James
Evans—" Here she pauses. The smile drops from her face as
the news sinks in. After a beat, she continues, "Was killed in
an automo—"[1] Her voice trails off. The camera cuts to the
Evans children, their faces reflecting disbelief at the crumbling
of life as they know it. Fade to black.

Throughout the next episode, Florida, newly widowed and shocked by her husband's untimely death and the loss of her dream of a new and better life for her family, busies herself taking care of funeral arrangements and everyone and everything around her. She dismisses the comfort loved ones try to offer her. In her performance, Emmy-award-winning and Golden Globe-nominated actress Esther Rolle paints a portrait of a black woman shouldering a tremendous emotional burden all by herself. Florida wears the mask of the unaffected. Unable to openly grieve or to show even those closest to her so much as the surface of the deep well of pain in which she's slowly drowning, she marches on, always strong, always self-contained, always stoic.

When they offer to help her clean the house, Florida snaps at her young adult children and they flee. Alone in the kitchen, she goes about wrapping leftovers and putting away dishes until, finally, she stops. A wave of emotion hits her, and she smashes a glass punch bowl to the floor. In that moment, Florida Evans utters one of the most memorable and quoted lines in television history, "Damn, damn, daaaaamn!"[2] Her children, hearing the noise, rush to her side and embrace their mother as she finally allows herself to feel the grief of her new widowhood. In the ensuing decades, that final line has been mocked, satirized, joked about, and made into memes. But what lies beneath it, what Esther Rolle so brilliantly embodied, is the myth of the strong black woman.

THE UNBREAKABLE BLACK WOMAN

For many people, the image of the strong black woman has the air of a compliment, presenting itself as the flipside of the "angry black woman" coin. "Black women aren't dangerous," it seems to say. Instead, we are warriors, so gifted with fortitude and resilience we need never express hurt, grief, or sadness. Since we never display such emotions, it stands to reason that we never actually feel them. Being a strong black woman can also mean the suppression of what are generally considered positive emotions. We cannot display too much joy, or happiness, or love. Someone so strong would rarely be so moved, and in many circles, it's considered unseemly to be overly expressive. Black women get the message that the larger American culture frowns on too much emotion of any kind from us.

This need to hide how we feel also has an element of self-protection inherent in it. For generations, displaying too much emotion could be dangerous for our ancestors. An enslaved woman didn't have the luxury of lying in bed and weeping at the death of her man, or the selling away of her children, or in the aftermath of her own violent rape by the plantation owner. She was expected to get back to working in the field, or cooking in the kitchen, or raising someone else's children, and to resist that expectation would mean brutal punishment. A black man who showed his anger at being denied the right to vote risked being tossed in jail or hung from a tree.

That danger didn't disappear with the end of slavery, the successes of the Civil Rights Movement, or the dawning of a new millennium. In 2015, when twenty-eight-year-old Sandra Bland was found hanged to death in a Waller County, Texas, jail cell, many people protested the injustice of her arrest and the suspicious circumstances of her death. At the same time, others claimed she shouldn't have reacted in any way to the rudeness of the state trooper who stopped her, a man who video evidence later proved had failed to follow procedure. People on that side of the argument claimed she should never have protested. In other words, her arrest and the cascade of events that followed and resulted in her death, were, in their opinion, her own fault. They saw the tragic end of her life as a consequence of her display of emotion.

Add to this prohibition on emotional display the fact that black women have never been given permission from society to be the "gentler sex." American culture has historically treated all women as less than men, but at the same time, white women of a certain class were characterized as needing protection and rescue. Where black women were supposed to be hard, white women were fragile. Sojourner Truth, born into slavery and, after her escape to freedom, a vocal anti-slavery activist, argued on behalf of black women everywhere to be seen as the women they were. "That man over there," she explained at the 1851 Women's Convention, "says that women need to be helped into carriages, and lifted over ditches, and to have the best place everywhere. Nobody ever helps me into carriages, or over mud-puddles, or gives me any best place! And ain't I a woman?"[3] Truth pointed out that white women were boxed out of the power structure, but black women weren't just boxed out. They had a boot on their necks and chains on their ankles and were expected to endure with a superhuman strength that would never be demanded of their white counterparts.

Even today, a display of emotion from a black woman next to the same display, under the same circumstances, from a white woman will often be interpreted differently, especially by white people. The white woman will be seen as upset, while her black counterpart will be seen as angry, irate, out of control. While the white woman will be seen as sad, the black woman will be seen as dramatic. Many black women have learned that, if we want to be taken seriously and find a place in polite society, we must wear a mask of calm acceptance regardless of the circumstances we face. By the same token, because the stereotype of the strong black woman lives on, we're also seen as people who should never need help. This, of course, makes it all the more difficult for us to ask for help when we need it. This standard set by white America became ingrained in much of black America, especially those of us who sought to assimilate or to emulate what they saw as valuable in white culture.

Sometimes, that stoicism displayed by the stereotypical strong black woman is a matter of survival. However, even when it isn't, we all too often expect it of each other. We live in a subculture of emotional dishonesty within a larger culture of emotional dishonesty. We pretend to be happy when we're in pain. We pretend to be angry when we're heartbroken. We pretend to be unaffected by traumatic events. From parental admonishments, like "You better not cry, or I'll give you something to cry for," to children mocking each other as crybabies and targeting for torment the child who dares show emotion, we learn from an early age to deny our true feelings. But when we run from, suppress, or cover up our emotions, we always pay a price.

THE COSTS OF EMOTIONAL DISHONESTY

For a long time, I used alcohol to silence my emotions. Had I continued to drink regularly and to excess, I have no doubt I would have suffered long-term negative effects. I would have paid a high price for continuing to bury my feelings about the traumas of my childhood. If I had continued down the same path, I would have sacrificed my physical, mental, and emotional wellbeing. I knew enough about food and exercise to keep looking good on the outside, but that didn't mean excessive alcohol consumption wasn't damaging my heart, my brain, my liver, my kidneys, and my womb. My toned body was a mask that covered my internal self-destruction.

At different times in my life, I've also used sex, food, weed, romantic relationships, and the accumulation of material things to not only hide my hurt but also present an image of myself as happy. Happiness, or the appearance of it, has become a measurement of success in modern culture, and yet, we have a romanticized idea of happiness. The media, including advertising and social media, does an incredibly effective job of convincing us that there's something out there in the future that will make us happy.

When you get those designer shoes or that Tesla or Porsche, you'll be happy. When you lose weight and fit those goal jeans that were too small when you bought them, you'll be happy. When you buy a house in the right zip code, you'll be happy. When you get with the right man, land the right job, or party harder than everybody else in the room, you'll be happy. This pursuit of a false image of happiness leaves us constantly comparing ourselves to other people and constantly falling short. Yet we're convinced it's easier to pursue this Instagram-ready version of happiness than it is to confront the hurt, deal with the things that have shaped our lives, and examine who we are when no one else is around. All too often, we'd rather look happy than do what it takes to be happy.

Nowhere is this false happiness more apparent than in Atlanta, Georgia, a reality show hotbed. I sometimes call the city, where I currently live, "the Home of the Thousandaire." When I moved here, it seemed like everyone around me was living a life of great material success, but it didn't take long to discover there was a lot of pretense going on. Don't get me wrong. Many people here are engaged in work that matters. There are plenty of people in this city who have achieved great things, built great wealth, and contributed to society in important ways. But it's also a place that puts a premium on looking like achievement.

Men barely avoiding eviction lease expensive sports cars and buy rounds of drinks for their acquaintances at the cigar bar. Women walk around in red-bottom shoes and carry five-thousand-dollar bags while they exist one missed paycheck away from total financial demise. They live falsified lives because it's easier than being honest. Their display of wealth is equated with material success, and material success is equated with happiness. This kind of thinking runs especially deep with people of color because we've been so traumatized that many of us have learned to equate our wellbeing with these adornments. It's within our control to accumulate the things that will make us look and feel like we're doing well, and so we exercise that control.

The bags, shoes, and cars have no inherent meaning, good or bad, and there's nothing wrong with wanting or buying the best you can afford. Your possessions can be a reflection of your good taste or even a way of loving yourself. Unfortunately, we too often focus on amassing more stuff in an effort to avoid dealing with what's going on inside of us. Materialism as a substitute for self-love and emotional health is so pervasive in our culture that Kanye West wrote about it in the 2009 song "All Falls Down," pointing out how many of us have replaced the love of self with the love of wealth.

I grew up in a home where we often turned to retail therapy to hide our problems. These days, you don't even have to leave the house to indulge in a spending spree. Just log on to your laptop or jump on your phone, and anything you could possibly want to buy is right at your fingertips. Clicking the buy button may seem harmless in the moment, but for many of us, the cost of emotional dishonesty is an empty bank account, a stack of credit card bills, and the shame and embarrassment that can come with bankruptcy and folks finding out that appearance of financial success was all just smoke and mirrors.

Some women choose a different cover for their real emotions. Rather than deal with what's going on inside their own heads and hearts, they hide behind the mask of "busy." They portray themselves as martyrs. They sacrifice themselves to the job, to their family, to the church, and to other people's needs, and they want everyone to know it. The constant complaining about how much they have to do allows them to garner sympathy, while a packed schedule allows them to avoid dealing with their emotional lives. They sacrifice their self-care and even their dignity because they barely have time to brush their teeth or take a shower. They never stop moving, so they never have to deal with what they're feeling. These women pay a price for the emotional dishonesty at the core of the story they're telling about their lives. In truth, slowing down would mean having to face themselves and what they're thinking and feeling. Instead, they keep running and doing until they end up burned out and resentful.

The ways to hide from what you feel are endless. Some women choose sex or unhealthy relationships to silence their emotions. Some eat to escape, while others use drugs or alcohol as a means to suppress sadness, guilt, grief, or hurt. Some rely on never-ending chaos and drama in their lives to distract them from feeling. Regardless of which mechanism you choose, there is always a cost to pretending you can opt out of feeling. Emotions, positive and negative, pleasant and unpleasant, are a natural part of the human experience. When you fail to allow yourself to experience, process, and express the full range of human emotions, your emotional growth becomes stunted. If a part of you isn't growing and evolving, it's dying, so after a lifetime of practicing emotional dishonesty, you forget how to fully experience even your most positive emotions.

Emotional dishonesty with yourself also makes it difficult to understand and relate to what the people around you are feeling. It's difficult to truly empathize with someone else's sadness when you never allow yourself to feel sad. It's hard to get swept up in someone else's joy when you constantly tamp down your own. This inability to connect on an emotional level damages relationships, leaving you isolated and alone.

Finally, there are the physical consequences of not allowing yourself to feel. Historically, our culture has a tradition of eating unhealthy foods for a variety of reasons. That tradition lives on partly because those high-fat, high-sugar foods dull your emotions. They help you slip into the proverbial food coma, so you don't have to feel. These are the same foods that contribute to obesity and all the lifestyle diseases associated with it. Many of the substances we use to silence our emotions—food, alcohol, drugs—are slowly killing us, but repressing your emotions also has a direct negative impact on your health. Even while you look on the outside like everything is fine, denying how you really feel can cause your blood pressure to rise to unhealthy levels and depress your immune system. Wearing the mask can cut your life short.

TRAUMA AND THE SUPPRESSION OF OUR EMOTIONS

As the executive director of the Steve and Marjorie Harvey Foundation, I was privy to a lot of personal information about our camp participants and their families. What I learned led me to question why we do the things we do, particularly why we engage in self-destructive behavior and pass on that behavior to the next generation. That experience led me to seek out research on why black people in particular show up the way we show up emotionally. It was through this seeking that I found the work of Dr. Joy Degruy. In her 2005 book, *Post Traumatic Slave Syndrome: America's Legacy of Enduring Injury and Healing*, Dr. Degruy argues that the effects of slavery and institutionalized racism on generations of black people resulted in generations of trauma, the impact of which continues today.

On the one hand, Dr. Degruy offers, that trauma caused black people to develop a high level of resilience. On the other hand, that trauma left us with the symptoms of post-traumatic stress disorder as a part of our culture and as a part of our DNA. We became emotionally flawed, scarred, traumatized people, who called upon a core strength to keep going. We learned to deny our emotions, but we developed a continual bounce-back game. It's a double-edged sword. The same trauma that bred resilience also bred an inability to grieve. It was embedded in our molecular structure. With our deep religious roots, we're often quick to refer to this legacy of trauma as a generational curse. It's a way to explain how we see the same patterns repeated from one generation to the next.

Unfortunately, many of us accept that curse as our reality. We never confront it or challenge it. We don't realize we have it in our power to break the curse, to stop the expression of those traumatized genes. We say, "The sins of the father will be visited on the son," as if it's beyond us to do anything about it. We don't stop to examine the role we play in it. We don't even understand why we attach our fears and anxieties and suppression of emotion to our children, and in the process, clip their wings. We're so afraid of our own power that we refuse to confront our demons, and as a result, we teach those coming up behind us to shortchange themselves in the same ways.

We work so diligently to keep ourselves safe that we block opportunities for expansion. We put safety above love. We put safety above growth. And we put safety above pushing ourselves to be the very best we can be. We guard our hearts in an effort to protect ourselves from the pain we've experienced in our own past and the trauma generations before us withstood. We focus so intensely on self-protection that we leave little room for self-expression, and we teach our children to do the same.

While the post-traumatic slave syndrome Dr. Degruy describes is complex, the good news is that your DNA is not your destiny. The overreactions, the quickness to anger, the unexplainable depression, and the constant anxiety often associated with post-traumatic stress disorder can all be overcome. However, that overcoming requires you to give yourself permission to feel. As black people, as women, as humans who are all connected to each other, we have to give ourselves and each other permission to grieve, to rejoice, to feel sadness and delight, and to express it all in constructive ways. To live fully, you have to be willing to take off the mask.

REDISCOVERING YOUR EMOTIONS

Learning to acknowledge and express your emotions lays the foundation for the next step—learning to manage your emotions in healthy ways. This journey requires you to connect to yourself on a deeper level. Most of us aren't given the skills to do so in childhood because our parents never learned to deal with their own feelings. We don't learn how to recognize, express, and process our emotions in school or as a part of higher education because most of our teachers and professors don't have that knowledge to pass on to us. People can't give us what they don't have, and the ability to process the best and the worst of your emotions in a healthy way isn't a common skill in most modern Western cultures.

My father once told me that, of all his children, "You're the daughter I never worry about." In his eyes, I was so strong that I didn't need the same kind of care someone else might need. While I'm sure he meant it as a compliment, it was based on the same falsehood that keeps so many of us stuck playing a role. He saw me as invulnerable because I wore a mask of invulnerability. I had to choose for myself to stop faking it and get help living an emotionally honest life. Once I decided I wanted emotional health and I was willing to do the work to get it, once I committed to the process, the Universe moved in alignment with my desire. The origin of the saying "When the student is ready, the teacher will appear" is unclear, but the truth of it has been proven over and over in my life.

Because I was ready to make a change, I found teachers all around me, from the books I was reading to strangers in line at the grocery store or in the parking lot at the gym. I discovered that the life preserver I needed had always been there, but I had to assist in my own rescue. People could keep throwing the flotation device at me, but I still had to reach out and grab it. You will have to do the same. No one can do the work for you. It comes down to you doing the work for your emotional healing. Make a decision that you deserve it and take an active role in getting it.

If, like many women, you've never felt like your emotions mattered, if you've heard all your life that your feelings are unimportant, challenge that belief. Question why your emotional life would be any less important than anyone else's and look at the ways that message was communicated to you. Examine how you've been covering your emotions and the price you've paid for that cover-up. Often, we deem ourselves unworthy of grieving because there's always someone who's going through something worse or because our lives are so filled with blessings. We deem ourselves unworthy of taking time to settle in, identify what we're feeling, and deal with it in a healthy way. But suffering is not a competition, and blessings don't mean you never feel hurt.

Choose carefully who you decide to share your pain with, especially in the beginning of this journey to feeling. The wrong response from a trusted friend or loved one can send you spiraling back to old habits of self-silencing. If you take a chance and reveal your hurt to a girlfriend and her response is, "Girl, just pray about it," then you might need someone else to talk to. If you try to talk to your mother about the wounds of your childhood and she tells you to just get over it, she may not be ready for the conversation. Remember your friend and your mother can't give you what they don't have, and there's always a risk that someone who doesn't have the emotional maturity you're seeking could later use your shared confidence against you. Openness with friends and family has its place, and I believe in the power of prayer, but the Divine has also given us other tools for healing. I've found that for the deeper healing of intense wounds, therapy is an invaluable and irreplaceable tool.

Suffering is not a competition, and blessings don't mean you never feel hurt.

THERAPY SAVED MY LIFE

Don't make the mistake of thinking therapy will be a quick fix. Just like you can't take off the extra pounds you put on over thirty or forty years by going to the gym and eating well for a couple of weeks, it's going to take longer than a couple of weeks to take off the emotional baggage you've been carrying for decades. You've been dragging it with you everywhere you go for so long it seems like it's supposed to be there. It's like a person who lives with chronic back pain and doesn't even realize she's been suffering until she gets the physical therapy she needs and experiences a pain-free moment for the first time in years. There's a moment of clarity that this is what health feels like, but she still has more work to do. Even when it hurts and even when she'd rather be doing something else, she has to keep going back and keep doing the exercises if she wants lasting results.

My early exposure to counseling didn't create a positive perception of it in my mind. When our parents divorced, my mom suggested my sister and I talk to our pastor about the situation and how we were experiencing it. We were teenagers, and we were friends with the pastor's son. No matter how cool I thought our pastor was, I didn't want to talk to him about my issues. Because he knew us and our family, I didn't believe he could be unbiased, and I immediately suspected he would judge me. In my mother's limited world view, any kind of therapy outside of pastoral counseling was unfamiliar and unacceptable. In fact, in my family, therapy was seen as something only crazy people did. Right after college, Karli and I mentioned to our dad that we thought we might need therapy. He told us, "Black people ain't got time for that," and the conversation was closed.

It wasn't until I saw some of my friends going to therapy and getting results that I realized I could do it. I watched my sister and her husband, Ben, use therapy to build a strong foundation for their relationship before they walked down the aisle. I was inspired by her commitment to the process and her willingness to make therapy a regular part of her life. I also realized I make time and find money for whatever I value enough to make time and find money to have in my life. I make time to work out, and I have no problem going to Lululemon to buy a pair of leggings that cost over one hundred dollars. I needed to place that kind of value on my emotional health. I needed to be willing to invest at least as much in my emotional healing as I invested in adorning myself and taking care of my physical health.

After my first few therapy appointments, I started journaling about my experiences, past and present, and the emotions they brought up in me. I committed to showing up for my weekly appointments and being real with my therapist, and slowly, my emotional life unfolded in front of me and I began to heal. Ultimately, I discovered that I'd spent much of the first three decades of my life hiding from my emotions. I had to acknowledge the fact that I grew up feeling abandoned by my father and that wound left me using everything from food to unhealthy relationships to try to fill the void created by his absence. I had to acknowledge that, as an adult, I now owned the life I was creating for myself and the results I was getting.

For most of my life, I suffered from entitlement, approval seeking, and unrelenting standards. Driven to make my parents proud of me, I always tried to do things the right way. I went to college and excelled. I went off to work in multiple industries and created an excellent reputation for myself in many business circles. For the most part, I walked a pretty straight and narrow path, and like many women who seek the approval of others, I always showed up dressed for the part I was supposed to play. I had all the right words to say. I played my role of obedience, hoping the boat wouldn't get rocked. I ensured everyone's comfort except my own. I suffered silently, all while hoping to save face with fake friends and salvage dead relationships.

Eventually, I grew tired of wearing a mask. I was no longer willing to apologize for who I was for the sake of the team. I no longer want to quell my very real feelings of hurt. The dis-ease of needing to please others had left me emotionally black and spiritually blue. It was time for a change. In the words of Future, it was time for "mask off." I was ready to step out of the boat of mediocrity, leaving behind those who weren't ready to walk on water with me.

In order to make that change in my life, I had to lose the story I was telling myself and take one hundred percent responsibility for my present life. I parted ways with the excuses, and I made a total commitment to heal my life from the inside out. In the end, I shed the emotional and physical weight of guilt, shame, and unforgiveness. This was not the cute stuff they show you on the Gram. It was the kind of ugly, intimate transformation that forces you to hold up a mirror and examine all the hard-to-reach places in your life to uncover what's going on there. Be patient with yourself as you do this work. It's hard and painful, but necessary.

Removing the mask and learning how to process your emotions in a healthy manner doesn't mean you have to put the rest of what you want in life on hold. However, while you secure the bag, I charge you to also ensure your healing.

Drop the ego and get the therapy you desperately need. It doesn't mean you're crazy; it makes you the superhero in your own life. Learn your limits and set clear boundaries. I promise you the good will remain and the rest will find its way out.

Let's be real. Healing work is not an IG post. Taking off the mask is hard. It takes real courage to get vulnerable enough to share your true self with a therapist or anyone else. The mask you wear is just a protective shield to cover who you are underneath. It covers your failures, your depression, and your shame. It covers your pain, but in doing so, it requires you to play small to avoid looking human or making other people uncomfortable. The more you show up as the fake version of yourself, the more you close yourself off to the richness and fullness the Universe has to offer you. It's challenging to change, but you don't have to do it alone.

After my parents divorced, I grew up watching my father on television, but not having a relationship with him left me scarred. I felt like I was never good enough, never pretty enough, never worthy of his affections. I carried those scars into my young adulthood, and in many ways, they crippled me. Although my father supplied my financial needs, he struggled to meet my emotional needs. In search of a father figure, I set out on a quest to find love from men who never measured up and often mimicked the same unavailable behavior of my missing father.

As with many little girls whose fathers never showed up for the family portrait or school performances, my abandonment issues affected my self-esteem. I learned early on how to deflect. As I buried my hurt deep inside, I became destructive and self-destructive, and I suffered internally. I found that deep hole could never be filled, and I couldn't be made whole until I peeled back all the layers that made up my sadness, my grief, and my need for my father's love.

Like many of my friends suffering in silence, I was told to get over it. "Black people don't have time to be depressed. Girl, you don't need therapy." When I finally made a full commitment to healing myself, I stopped listening to those voices. I didn't go to therapy because it was the trending topic. I went because I was tired of feeling angry. I was exhausted and done with being triggered by indecipherable text messages from my father. I was sick and tired of being emotionally manipulated by men who latched their claws into my brokenness when, due to my emotional frailties, I was too weak to fight them off.

Trust me when I tell you it got ugly before it got cute. I wrote letters, I starved relationships, and I shed so many tears. (Cue Tupac.) I looked myself in the mirror and had honest talks about who I was, what I wanted, and how I wanted to live my life going forward. I promised myself freedom. Every week my North Star was that therapist's couch. Therapy saved my life.

Healing is on the other side of your traumas, but you must be willing to go beyond to confront them head-on. I'm a much better woman, sister, daughter, friend, and business owner because of my willingness to open my wounds so they could be treated and finally mend. In order for more people to get that same kind of healing, we must remove the stigma surrounding mental health issues and therapy in our community. In the words of mental health advocate Shanti

Das, we must "silence the shame" so we can all, each one of us, get the help we so desperately need.

We're often told to take our burdens to the Lord and leave them there. However, I'm of the belief that every single one of us, male or female and of any race or religion, can benefit from therapy. Give yourself the opportunity to find a qualified therapist and work with her or him to do the deep work. Heart work is hard work, and there's nothing like having an unbiased ally who can support you in getting it done. Be willing to go through the pain to get to your power. Be willing to look at your life and the choices you've made with clear eyes and without judgment. Be willing to take off the mask and look at the real you—in all her hurt, pain, wonder, and beauty—underneath.

MANAGE YOUR EMOTIONS

When you open the door to your own emotions, you also have to be willing to open the door to the emotions of the people in your life. Meet them head on, but without conflict. This starts with doing your own work first, so you can meet your mother, your man, your sister, or your child with compassion, not from a place of anger or resentment and not from a place of martyring yourself to the other person's feelings. That connection with yourself will give you the ability to avoid taking anyone else's feelings personally. Be willing to listen and understand even if you don't agree. Adult people talk to each other. Adults express their emotions in constructive ways. Adults allow each other to feel.

Recently, an acquaintance made some comments that offended me. In the following days, I found myself thinking I didn't want to be around her anymore. I just wanted to avoid her altogether, and in the past, I might have done that. I might even have confronted her in anger. Instead, I picked up the phone and called and asked her exactly what she'd meant by what she said. We discussed the situation, and she explained that she had misspoken. We were able to talk through our differing opinions on the subject and move on. That kind of directness doesn't always work out the way you want it to. My acquaintance could've had a completely different reaction. She could have gotten upset and indignant with me for even questioning her intentions. She could've responded in anger. In that case, it would've been up to me to manage my response. I would've let the relationship go, knowing I had done my part in trying to reach an understanding.

Learning to manage your emotions is part of functioning as a healthy, mature adult. You can't wish for a happy life and then go around spewing anger at the world. You're responsible for your life. You're not, however, responsible for other people's feelings or actions. Your parents' story is not your story. You don't have to be who other people say you are. You don't have to play the victim, the martyr, or the savior in anyone's story. If that's been you up until now, it doesn't have to be you anymore. You can be a strong woman and still ask for help. You can learn to live in the fullness of your human experience regardless of what's going on around you. You can feel it all and come out stronger for it.

Affirmation

I AM SAFE.
I AM LOVED.
I AM PROTECTED.

Affirmation

**I DESERVE TO LIVE
A LIFE OF TRUTH.**

3

EMBRACE THE
REAL BOSS LIFE

I N 2018, I WAS HONORED to receive an award for
Boss Woman of the Year in the "Spiritual Warrior" category. That evening, for the first time, I spoke publicly
about Christ consciousness and how I've come to a new
understanding of divinity, including the divinity within all
of us, the divinity within me. Some of the women seemed
uncomfortable, and I wondered if I'd launched this new
material with the wrong audience. Perhaps, I thought, I should
have waited until I was in a different space to talk about
something that invited women to challenge their long-held
beliefs. But after the event ended, a group of women lined up
to talk with me. One by one, they explained that I'd given
them exactly what they needed that day. They'd needed a
license to question what they'd been taught. They'd needed
confirmation that they weren't crazy for searching YouTube
videos to find out how to discover the spirituality that had

been missing in their experience of religion. They'd needed someone to raise her hand and go first.

The sun hadn't yet risen when I boarded a plane to return to Atlanta the next morning. As I looked out into the darkness, the thoughts running through my mind since the night before crystalized. The real boss life, I realized, isn't defined by how big your business can grow. My own business was in its infancy. It can't be achieved by posting your annual revenues or screenshotting your Shopify account to prove you had a six-figure month. I was still working to become profitable. It can't be measured in dollars and cents, numbers of employees, or material results. By those standards, I hadn't yet achieved many of my own goals.

Contrary to what we see on social media, the real boss life is creating an avenue for people to break free of whatever has been holding them back. Because I had found my way to freedom, I was able to give someone else access to that same thing in her own life. I was able to give scores of women in the room what they needed to hear that night. I was able to be of service. I do it every week, when I send newsletters that reveal the light and dark of my journey. I do it when I invite women to come and work out at my gym. I do it when I demonstrate calm in the face of conflict and confrontation not just for my own benefit but as a model of the possibility that you can learn to manage your emotions. The real boss life is never about the boss. The real boss life requires us to serve.

We live in a self-focused culture. It's the age of the selfie and self-promotion. All over social media, people self-proclaim their own greatness. *Look what I bought. Look what I did. Look at me.* The strategically placed Chanel bag just happens to show up in the background of a picture. The Rolls Royce logo is on display on the headrest as the business guru livestreams about her latest success story. And #bosslife #bossup #bossbitch are slapped on the posts so we all start to believe a "boss life" is defined by nothing more than what you can acquire. But nothing could be further from the truth.

Although I've sometimes strayed from this truth, I've always known it, and I've always come back to it. When I was a first-year student at Hampton University, the dean of students met with all the political science majors. One by one, we introduced ourselves and explained what we wanted to do with our lives. In the room were aspiring criminal defense attorneys, entertainment lawyers, and politicians. As I waited my turn, I knew none of those career paths were for me. When I finally introduced myself, I said, "My name is Brandi Harvey. I'm from Cleveland, Ohio. And I want to change the world."

At seventeen years old, I couldn't put a finger on exactly what changing the world would look like, but as I've grown and matured, I've chosen every career move I've made with that purpose. Many times, I was a volunteer, changing the world without compensation, but those experiences paid off in dividends, allowing me to develop my raw talent and strengthen my leadership skills. They made me a better speaker, business owner, and leader. They made me a better person. Sometimes, the real boss life means showing up and giving of yourself even when there's no paycheck involved.

Over the years, I've led afterschool programs, worked as a fitness instructor, taught high school, run a charitable foundation, and organized mentoring programs. I launched Beyond Her, my active wellness site for black women, as my platform for changing the world on a larger scale. When I was a young girl listening to Les Brown's motivational speeches, I had no idea what his job was, but I knew I wanted to do what he did. Now, I motivate, inspire, and enlighten audiences. I'm changing the world with my words and my transparency and by sharing my journey and what I've learned along the way.

Early on, I recognized how we can change the world by starting right where we are. When I enter a space, I intentionally bring goodness. I change the atmosphere for the better. That's a real boss, someone who can shift the energy of a room and make things better no matter where she goes. Rather than reflecting the temperature of the room, you set the temperature. You exert your influence for the betterment of everyone involved. When you acquire new knowledge, you share it. In an interview with *O, The Oprah Magazine,* Nobel laureate Toni Morrison said, "I tell my students, 'When you get these jobs that you have been so brilliantly trained for, just remember that your real job is that if you are free, you need to free somebody else. If you have some power, then your job is to empower somebody else. This is not just a grab-bag candy game.'"[4] That's a boss, someone who recognizes success is never just about the one who succeeds. When you get free, you free somebody else.

GIVE FROM THE OVERFLOW

The real boss life requires you to be willing to give of yourself. However, it doesn't require that you give until it hurts or drain yourself until you have nothing left. Serving with your gifts isn't an excuse to martyr yourself. You may have heard the saying that you can't pour from an empty cup, meaning you can't give when you're completely empty. The idea is that you must keep some amount of resources for yourself. However, I'd like to invite you to take that metaphor a step further. Think instead of a cup sitting on a saucer. When you pour into the cup until it's filled and keep pouring, it will eventually overflow, and the liquid will spill into the saucer. That extra, what's spilled over, is what you have to offer the world. You can serve not just without depleting yourself but while making sure your needs are met. You deserve for your cup to remain as close to full as possible at all times.

Most of us never take the time to hit the refresh button on our lives. We become overloaded, but we continue to take on what we think we must, and the results are rage, aggression, and outbursts. Our grandmothers and mothers didn't prioritize self-care. They were the carriers of the family's burdens, the neighbors' burdens, the church's burdens, and so we have no examples of what self-care looks like. Our examples are of women who constantly put themselves third, fourth, or last. The only relief they found was in church, and two or three hours on Sunday morning just wasn't enough to restore and replenish them. They worked themselves into illness, broken relationships, a miserable existence, and too often, an early grave because they rarely had—or took— enough time to just be.

It's your responsibility to fill your own cup. You cannot allow yourself to get tapped out emotionally, physically, and financially and then throw tantrums because you expect other people to make up for what you lack. You can't deplete your own reserves and then demand that your sisters, friends, and daughters give to you from theirs. No one owes you that. You owe it to yourself to make sure you don't get down to empty, and if you do, to course correct and get back into balance.

Regular self-care is at the heart of filling your cup, and having a self-care routine requires you to take a stance for your own wellbeing. This is often especially difficult for black women because we're taught by the culture and by the examples in our lives that so many other people and things are more important than our own needs. But you have to love yourself as much as you love the people you've put ahead of yourself in the past. You can't afford to wait until you have more time or more money—after you've taken care of everyone else—to commit to your self-care. If you need to get away to a spa or on a vacation, then adjust your schedule and your budget to do that, but realize that self-care is always within reach. It could be as simple as allowing yourself peace and quiet, with no interruptions, in a designated space in your house.

Find simple ways to honor your mind, body, and spirit every day. When you do, your family will thrive. Your emotional outbursts will cease, and you will mend or release relationships with minimal effort. When we all commit to self-care, we'll truly have black love in our families. We will stay together because we'll be well together.

I can't tell you what your self-care routine should look like. You have to discover what nourishes you and gives you peace. What you put into your body is a part of your self-care. Whether you choose to decompress with a glass of wine or by sitting in silence for a few minutes is a self-care decision. Meditation and exercise are self-care. Turning off the TV and reading something that feeds your mind or your spirit is self-care. Getting out of bed and taking a shower when it feels impossible is self-care. Going out in nature and being present to the sound of the wind in the leaves and birds greeting each other in the distance, going to bed so you can get a full night's sleep, turning off your phone and driving to work in silence—these are all acts of self-care.

SET BOUNDARIES

In 2017, I started setting real boundaries for myself. That year, for the first time in my life, I spent Thanksgiving alone. I made that decision to protect my energy and take care of my own needs. I chose to stay in my own home and enjoy solitude. I didn't want to rush to be anywhere just because society dictates that I should spend Thanksgiving with family or friends.

In the past, I would have run myself ragged trying to do everything for Twin Pop, the business I ran with my sister at that time, and meet everyone's personal needs at the same time. Choosing not to go home to Cleveland for the holiday was my way of honoring my own needs in that moment, even though they conflicted with other people's desires. In that quiet place, I thought a lot about purpose and destiny—the two words echoing over and over in my thoughts when I woke up alone on Thanksgiving Day—and I realized that they always require sacrifice. Yes, it was something of a sacrifice not to spend the holiday with my family, but it was a sacrifice in alignment with my purpose, my destiny, and my needs.

Learning to set boundaries in my personal and professional life has been a process for me. In my first few years as executive director of the foundation, I'd tried to do it all. It took me a few years to learn the value of bringing in capable help, delegating important tasks, and saying no when I needed to say it. I had to learn that "no" is a complete sentence. It doesn't require explanation. This was also a lesson I had to learn in my relationships with men. I had to set up boundaries around my heart and my emotions to protect myself. In the past, I'd treated my heart as consumable by the men I was involved with. They had total access to me, physically, mentally, and emotionally, and I was the one left depleted while they went about their lives. I was depleted because I allowed myself to be an open vessel.

That all changed when I realized I'm a power source. Every time someone connects to me, I give them energy, life, inspiration, and empowerment. I was pouring from my cup because I thought I had a full cup. I thought my cup overflowed, and I was uplifting everyone else so they would have enough. In reality, my own cup wasn't filled, and I was left feeling depressed, anxious, sad, lonely, and inadequate. You are a power source, but you can't allow that power to be tapped into indiscriminately. You have to set boundaries— like a boss—to ensure you first meet your own needs, fuel yourself, take care of you, fill your cup to the brim, and then give what you have left where you see fit to give it.

When I didn't have boundaries in my life it was because I didn't really know or acknowledge what my heart desired. I said I didn't care if I got married or not, for example, but in reality, I wanted a monogamous relationship and to ultimately be married. Because I wasn't clear about what I wanted, I tolerated people and things that were never going to get me to my goals. Finally, I began to ask myself what made me feel loved, what made me feel safe, and what made me feel protected. I honored my spirit by saying yes to those things and no to everything else.

Take responsibility for your lack of boundaries by saying what you really mean and really meaning what you say. If you say yes to something, say it wholeheartedly and for reasons that make sense to you. And if your answer is no, say it without need for apology or explanation. Care for your personal space by deciding who will be in it and who will not. Understand that your time is precious, and when you choose to give it, that choice should be intentional. A real boss dictates where her time and energy will be spent.

You don't have to make a big announcement on social media or call people and tell them you're no longer tolerating their infringing on your resources. You don't have to say, "I'm not giving you my time anymore." The only person who needs to know you're setting these new boundaries is you. Simply choose to no longer enter certain spaces, to stop inviting certain people, to stop responding to certain posts or text messages. Stop entertaining conversations designed to lead you to your demise. Create distance between you and the people who trigger you, and unfollow the people whose posts anger you.

Yes, it can be difficult to set boundaries. It's a skill I'm still practicing. In fact, before I went to therapy, I didn't even know I lacked appropriate boundaries in my life. I had to be told. I had to learn how to set boundaries because I didn't have examples in my own life of people who set healthy boundaries in theirs. But this work is important enough to learn how to do it, and to do it even when it's hard. If you fail to set boundaries, you'll end up with the life someone else wants you to have. You'll have the friendships and romantic relationships other people want to give you. You'll spend your life doing the work someone else wants you to do. You'll lose yourself to other people's needs.

Because of our relationship issues, our daddy issues, our mama issues, our low-self-esteem and insufficient self-love, our lack of trust in ourselves, and our fears, we fail to set boundaries. But when you realize you're the power source and your life is worth the effort of constructing boundaries, as uncomfortable as that work can sometimes be, your "no" becomes non-negotiable. You get clear about where you will not go and what you will not tolerate in your life. When you get clear about what you don't want, it's much easier to know what you do want. You learn to trust yourself. Your emotional, spiritual, and physical availability become treasured assets you protect.

> **If you fail to set boundaries, you'll end up with the life someone else wants you to have.**

Getting the breakthrough you desire requires you to redefine what it means to be a boss. Be willing to give of yourself and use your gifts to serve, creating value for others, while still taking care of your own needs and nurturing your body, mind, and spirit. Master the art of setting boundaries and deciding where you'll invest your time and energy and what you'll walk away from to protect your own wellbeing. Become the real boss of your own life.

Affirmation

I AM CONFIDENT THAT
MY NO WILL MAKE ROOM
FOR THE YES I DESERVE.

4 GET IN FIGHTING SHAPE

ONE AFTERNOON, I STOPPED FOR lunch at a local health food restaurant, and while I was enjoying a kale salad and a green juice, a young black woman walked in. Like so many women, she was overweight (as I used to be), but she was talking on her phone, telling the person on the other end how she was working on losing weight and getting in shape. I waited for an opening, and when she hung up the phone, I smiled and waved her over to my table. "You don't know me," I said, "but I overheard a little of your conversation, and I'd like to invite you to come to my gym." I explained to her that E.F.F.E.C.T. Fitness, in Southwest Atlanta, is a welcoming, supportive place for people at every level of fitness, a place where people get results. She graciously accepted my intrusion and the information I gave her. She might have been cussing me out in her head. She might have left the restaurant thinking people need to mind their own business. But I want for her and for all women the freedom

I've found from getting into fighting shape, and I can't help sharing the resources I've discovered on my path to wellness.

Admittedly, I have a "drill sergeant" reputation among my friends when it comes to health and fitness. Everybody knows I draw clear lines about what I will and will not put into my body. They all know I go hard in the gym, but they also know I don't judge where other people are on their journey to health. Instead, I openly share everything I've learned about wellness. My audacity in sharing the benefits of moving your body is motivated by my desire to see more people, and especially more women of color, open their eyes to how much control we have over our own lives. I feel fortunate to have discovered that power early in my life.

If you stumbled upon the Fountain of Youth, you wouldn't keep that natural wonder to yourself. You'd want everyone you loved and cared about to drink from its waters. That's how I feel about what I've learned over the years about food, exercise, and the mind-body-spirit connection. It's my duty to share that knowledge and to challenge the women in my life to level up to where I know they can be. When my mother comes to town, we go to the gym and work out together. When I see my sister at the gym, I encourage her to take an extra class. I tell strangers in the grocery store why I eat plant-based. I want longevity for myself, and I want it for everyone around me. I picture a generation of centenarians still walking and running, gardening and painting, learning and creating. They look good and feel good until the end of their lives. I want to make that vision a reality.

That conversation in the health food restaurant wasn't unusual for me. I'm constantly inviting friends, family, and random strangers to try my gym. It's one of those secrets I feel called to share, so much so that people often think I'm pitching my own business. In reality, I just work out there. I don't own a gym. Instead, I created Beyond Her, my lifestyle brand, as an active wellness destination for women of color. I want women like me to understand they have as much right to wellness as anyone else. Life doesn't just happen to us. We are active participants in our healing and our wellness.

Most of us have forgotten that we are healers. We all have the power to heal ourselves. Our ancestors went into the garden and dug up roots and picked leaves to cure indigestion or a headache. They enjoyed a connection with nature and natural health that we've largely lost in modern culture. Today, the black woman with flawless skin and excellent health, who understands which plants heal and nourish her body, is portrayed in the movies and on TV as a nearly mythical being. She lives all alone in a cabin in the woods, and no one understands her power. In fact, people fear her as much as they marvel at her abilities. She adorns her hair with crystals and shells, and rather than waiting for an anointing, she anoints her own body with oil infused with herbs she forages from the bounty that surrounds her. She is at once beautiful and primitive. She's a mystic, a witch doctor, a voodoo priestess. She is, for purposes of entertainment, reduced to a curiosity, someone the hero turns to when he can't get help anywhere else.

Pull back the layers on that image, and you find a well-hidden truth. You have the same power as the woman in the woods. Natural health and healing are birthrights we've given up over centuries because we've been told the old ways are primitive and ineffective. We've substituted the judgment of doctors in white lab coats for our own instinctive knowing. We've traded healthy living for the quick-fix solutions cooked up by the pharmaceutical complex that has all too often used us as guinea pigs. Under the pretext of meeting our nutritional needs, we put death into our bodies, and the end result is acne and autoimmune disease, depression, anxiety, high blood pressure, diabetes, cancer, and death.

When Jesus walked this Earth, he said, "I came that you might have life and have it more abundantly." In the physical, that includes abundant health and vitality. That means the ability to wake up free from pain and go through life without the fear that a heart attack or a stroke will be a part of your future. That means enjoying life to the fullest because your body functions the way it was designed to function. It means physical wellbeing that allows you to create excellence in every area of your life.

I haven't always enjoyed a healthy lifestyle. Growing up, I ate the black folks' version of the standard American diet. However, I started to become conscious of what I was putting into my body as a young adult. It was the beginning of my commitment to health. The full transition would take years, but it was ignited, in a single moment, by a comment my father made. It was our sophomore year in college, and Karli and I had gone to visit him for spring break. During that visit, he took a look at us and said, "I see my girls are getting fluffy."

"Fluffy! What the f-ck?" we said. My sister laughed it off, and on the outside, so did I. But our father's words echoed in my mind for the rest of the visit. *Seriously?* I kept thinking.

Did my dad call me fat? Frankly, the words hurt. My relationship with my him was already strained. At that age, I still felt a deep sense of abandonment from his long absences during my childhood. I was angry with my dad for not being there for me, but I was still a little girl who wanted his love and approval.

It would've been easy to think he was being too critical of me and blame him for having the nerve to say something about my weight. It would have been easy to take "fluffy" as an insult, allow it to hurt me, and then go off and eat some more to silence my hurt feelings. If I were a more carefree woman, his words might have gone in one ear and out the other. If I were less resilient, my father's words might have crushed me. Instead, his casual comment pissed me off. As much as it hurt my feelings, it also hurt my pride. I wanted to prove he was wrong about me, and in pursuit of that goal, I started on a journey to fitness and health that would last a lifetime.

It wasn't like I hadn't already noticed my weight gain. I had to struggle into the same size twelve jeans that had always fit just fine, and bending over to tie my shoes actually hurt. That's not "normal" for someone who isn't even twenty years old yet. But it was normal for most of the people around me, and I had more or less accepted it. My dad putting words to it drove home the point that something was out of order with the way I was treating my body. He had thrown down the gauntlet, but he would never have the opportunity to call me fat again. I wanted to make him eat his words, but I also wanted him to be proud of how I took them as an invitation to level up and get fit. He had awakened the sleeping giant within me.

My "fluffy" moment came at the perfect time. Karli and I had recently transferred to Ohio State. I didn't know many people on campus yet, and I decided to go into the new school year looking like my best self. My dorm room was right across from the Jesse Owens Recreational Center, and I made use of it as soon as I got back to school. Interestingly, our father's comment hadn't really impacted Karli, and she had no interest in working out—until she saw me losing weight. We'd spent our whole lives looking just alike, but as I lost weight, that changed. It had always been obvious that we were twins, but people started to ask if we were sisters. Karli decided she didn't want to be the fat twin, and she joined me in the gym. However, it wasn't an overnight transformation for either us, especially since we knew next to nothing about nutrition. After our workouts, we'd go out for milkshakes, but we were young, and we lost weight easily.

The next time my father saw me, he was shocked. "You look like you need a sandwich!" he told me, and in that moment, I felt like I'd won. I had dropped all that extra fat and put on muscle, but I had also started what would become a way of life for me. I doubt if any of that would've happened at that point in my life without the kick in the ass he gave me that spring day. Most people are afraid of telling each other the truth. We tiptoe around each other and let the people we care about exist in the fake realities they create for themselves. I'm grateful that my dad spoke a truth I needed to hear. While neither of us had known it at the time, he ignited a change in me that would positively impact every facet of my life.

Even though I lost weight quickly and never regained it, my knowledge about physical health was still limited. Our culture is so far removed from natural ways of nourishing and moving our bodies and healing ourselves that it takes time to recover your birthright—a truly healthy, functional, and fit body. This journey to health and fitness is a lifelong one, but it's worth taking. Mine started in college, but I still had a lot to learn, and it would take me years to discover a true and reliable path.

CONSCIOUS EATING

When I was a freshman in college, I had a professor named Dr. Lee. He was vegan, wore his hair locked, and was always eating fruit. I thought this man was the epitome of strange. One day during a class discussion, Dr. Lee explained why he didn't eat anything that had parents or any animal byproducts. He also expressed that he never chewed gum or used conventional deodorant because they contained chemicals that were known to cause cancer.

Sitting in the back of the class, I laughed at him, thinking he was a complete joke. After he completed his laundry list of things he didn't eat, I raised my hand. Hoping to get a laugh out of the class, I asked sarcastically, "So what do you eat?" His response was simple, "I eat food." There I sat with the dumbest look on my face. The joke was on me.

I walked back to my dorm thinking the man was a complete idiot. I thought about all the ways I could withdraw from his class because Dr. Lee obviously wasn't equipped to teach me. The man didn't eat meat, use regular deodorant, or chew gum. What was wrong with him? I would much rather die, gripping my grease-soaked box of Popeye's, than be subjected to the teachings of a man who had lost his mind and his taste buds.

Fast forward seventeen years, and here I am with locked hair. I use natural deodorants and don't eat anything that had parents. It's incredible how time will teach us all the things we have to lose to win in our lives. Dr. Lee and his beliefs had seemed so foreign to me as a teenager. But the more I became committed to my health and wellness, the more I read about the effects of food on our bodies. In the process, I uncovered all the dangerous chemicals and cancer-causing ingredients that can render our body products, environment, and food supply toxic. Dr. Lee was right all along.

I'm often asked the same question I asked Dr. Lee, and when I answer, many people tell me all the things they could never give up or let go of in their lives. They say they'd much rather die happy and satisfied than live deprived. I smile and nod, thinking of how I shared those beliefs once upon a time. Never in a million years would I have thought I'd be living a plant-based lifestyle. When I started down this path years ago, it was rocky. I couldn't fully commit, and I fell off numerous times and worried that I might not be disciplined enough to see it through. But I didn't quit.

Dr. Lee planted a seed in my life that took time to blossom. Over the years, I had to lose my ego, my beliefs about health, and the way I showed love to myself. Losing these things didn't take anything away from me. It added more to who God was calling me to be. I realized the animal products most of us grow up eating have been linked to many of the health problems we want to avoid. Fruits and vegetables and seeds and nuts, on the other hand, provide all the macronutrients and micronutrients our bodies need. I decided that if I wanted to fulfill the higher purpose God designed me to fulfill, I had to feed my body in a way that will sustain a long and healthy life.

Changing how I ate wasn't primarily about looks or weight loss. It was about energy, vitality, and longevity. It's easy to think that people who look fit and trim must be eating well and healthier than the average person. However, that's often not the case. In my short time as a fitness competitor, I ate what most people in that world eat, a diet high in animal protein and extremely low in carbs. I took in all kinds of chemicals and fake foods. I chewed sugar-free gum all day because my hunger never went away. I drank whey protein shakes. I weighed and measured all of my food. Of course, I got lean, but I couldn't use the bathroom. My poop was like pellets. I drank a gallon or two of water every day, but I didn't take in enough fiber, only found in plants, to regularly move my bowels. My abs were popping, but my body wasn't functioning the way it was designed to function. I had cystic acne, and I was constantly breaking out. To top it off, I was angry all the time, snapping at anybody and everybody. However, I was driven by my goal of winning a fitness competition, and nothing else mattered.

One day at the gym, I felt myself blacking out. I was supposedly in the best physical condition of my life, and I was seeing stars and trying not to pass out. It scared me enough that I started researching all the processed food I was eating. I discovered the controversial history of artificial sweeteners. I read about the fat-free, high-sugar craze of the 1980s and how it resulted in weight gain for millions of people and a spike in obesity rates. I learned that the idea that fat makes us fat is a lie. Our bodies require high quality fats to function at the highest level, and those fats don't come from dead animals.

If you ask me the healthiest way to eat, I'm going to steer you to plant-based eating every single time. If you ask me the best way to lose weight, I'll still tell you to go eat plants—not for a month but for a lifetime. I had shed my excess body fat years before I gave up animal products, and I was no longer "fluffy," but I was able to easily maintain that fat loss and continue to put on muscle with plant-based eating. I also saw incredible improvements in my overall health.

At first, it was hard for me. I didn't mind cutting out the meat, but I hated giving up desserts. Unfortunately, most desserts are made with milk, butter, and eggs, all of which are, of course, animal products. So I started off my plant-based life making an exception for dessert. I wouldn't buy any animal products or eat them in my home, but I'd happily make an exception when I was eating out. Whenever anyone tried to call me on it, I'd tell them dessert didn't count. "Dessert isn't meant to be vegan," I'd say. "It's supposed to have whipped cream on it."

I went plant-based for up to six months at a time, but inevitably, I'd decide I wanted to try something different or just have a piece of fish again because I felt like it in the moment. For a few years, it was start and stop for me. Even though I knew plant-based eating was the best choice for me, I wasn't fully committed to giving up meat, poultry, seafood, and dairy products. I knew it was the right choice for the kind of life I wanted to live, but I told myself it was too hard to really stick with it. Finally, at the beginning of 2016, I realized I'd been playing at this new lifestyle choice, and it was time for that to change.

Plants are the primary source of almost all the micro-nutrients—vitamins and minerals—you need for health and longevity. These are the naturally occurring substances that provide protection from inflammation and disease. Plants provide you with fiber, which is necessary for proper digestion and which you can't get in meat, dairy, or eggs. Over time, I began to see animal products, especially meat, for what they were—death on a plate. It seemed ridiculous to me to try to build life by consuming death.

Those of us who grew up in church learned that the body is a temple, but typically, that was preached about in reference to "sinful" things like drugs and sex. If your body is a temple when it comes to who you sleep with, it's still a temple when you're standing in line at an all-you-can-eat buffet, and you need to treat it as such. Your body is still a temple when you're pouring a two-liter bottle of cola into it. Your body is still a temple when you're feeding it the fear and adrenaline that went through that animal's body as it was led to slaughter.

As children, we're taught "you are what you eat." Understand that when you eat meat, you also eat everything that animal has eaten. Much of the seafood available for purchase has been contaminated by mercury, lead, PCBs, or other harmful chemicals. You can get a list of which fish are likely to have the lowest levels of contaminants, but the smarter choice is to avoid putting contaminants in your body. Other animals, including chickens and turkeys, but especially large animals like cows and pigs, may be exposed to antibiotics, synthetic hormones, pesticides, and environmental toxins before they're wrapped in plastic and stored in the refrigerator case of your local grocery store. While some of these are lawfully administered to the animals, they're not products I want to put into my body. Most of the animals raised for slaughter live in close quarters, where they're surrounded by their own feces and exposed to their diseased and even dead and decaying counterparts. None of this is a part of the recipe for your health.

Many people thinking of going plant-based happily give up meat but don't want to let go of cheese on their sandwich or milk for their coffee. We're raised to drink our milk because our parents are taught that we won't have strong bones and teeth unless we do. While the dairy industry in this country runs ads that promote milk as a healthy and necessary part of a balanced diet, several studies say otherwise. Other research has shown that about sixty-five percent of adults have a diminished capacity to digest lactose as they grow out of infancy. The percentage is higher in certain ethnic groups.[5]

Since milk is a substance that mammals, including humans, produce to feed their babies, it makes sense that babies would be able to digest the milk from their mothers. What doesn't make sense is to continue consuming something you can't properly digest. As a kid, I ate as much dairy as anyone else, even though it consistently gave me a scratchy throat, clear evidence that I had a dairy allergy. Someone with a severe peanut allergy might go into anaphylactic shock and struggle to breathe after eating one peanut. My reaction wasn't so dramatic, and because I'd experienced it all of my life, I saw it as normal. As I got older, that itchy throat was accompanied by constant breakouts and cystic acne, but once I cut out all dairy products, those symptoms went away. We've been led to believe that we can't get enough calcium without consuming dairy. In reality, beans, sesame seeds, leafy greens, like collards and kale, broccoli, and many other plant foods provide calcium in plentiful amounts.

It's no secret that an obesity epidemic has hit much of the Western world, including the United States. According to the Centers for Disease Control and Prevention, in 2017 more than thirty-nine percent of adults were obese.[6] The problem was even worse for black women over twenty years old, fifty-six percent of whom were obese.[7] And those percentages were trending upward. Take that number in and understand what it means. Essentially, half of black women are not just overweight but obese.

Reversing that trend isn't about forcing all women to fit a particular esthetic. The number on a clothing label is irrelevant. My concern is that many of the women in my community are carrying around so much excess fat that it's slowly killing them. We can dress it up in a cute outfit, a beat face, and a fly haircut, but obesity is still devastating our community. We are literally eating ourselves to death with high rates of heart attack, stroke, diabetes, high blood pressure, and cancer. It's one thing to embrace a curvy figure, it's something else to encourage behavior that's destroying lives.

Obesity-related diseases are largely preventable but common causes of death. For the small percentage of people who eat the standard American diet and aren't yet overweight, the results are still the same. They may not wear their poor diet on the outside, but the damage is being done to their organs. Even if the lifestyle diseases don't kill you, they set you up for a lifetime of living less than the life you were purposed to live. You cannot be at your best when you're dragging through each day. You cannot be at your best when your sex drive has dried up and disappeared. You cannot be at your best when you're dependent on a daily fistful of pills to function.

As a society, we rarely discuss the fact that being overweight and obesity can also result in increased risk of reproductive health issues in both women and men. Infertility, difficulty conceiving, rates of miscarriage, and pregnancy complications all increase when a woman is overweight or obese. Even with medical interventions, like *in vitro* fertilization, many of these women will still struggle to get pregnant. Whether you want to have children or not, you shouldn't lose the option because of what you put in your mouth. Your food should support your health, not rob you of it. The good news is that many of these conditions can be alleviated or reversed with healthy lifestyle changes, including a plant-based diet.

TRANSITIONING TO PLANT-BASED EATING

One of the most widely believed myths about plant-based eating is that it doesn't provide enough protein. But most people who eat a typical American diet actually consume more protein, in the form of dead animals, than they need. Search for vegan bodybuilders and fitness competitors online and look at their pictures. They're as big, as cut, and as fit as their chicken-eating competitors. In fact, more and more professional athletes are choosing a vegan diet. Many go vegan because they discover the diet supports injury rehabilitation much better than the conventional diets they grew up eating, or the old training diets. Others do it to drop body fat, so they can be leaner and faster. Fueled by plants, they're competing at the highest levels. They find their protein in nuts and seeds, rice and beans, quinoa, leafy greens, and other plant sources. A lack of protein isn't a concern when you eat a varied plant-based diet.

A lot of people turn up their noses at plant-based eating because they expect it to be bland and boring. If you've spent a lifetime eating fried foods and lots of cheese, food products manufactured in a lab to excite your taste buds, and heaps of sugar and salt added to your meals, then yes, your first kale salad will probably taste plain to you. But your palate will adjust over time. The more fruits and vegetables you eat, the better they'll taste. In the meantime, you can be just as creative in the kitchen with vegetables as you ever were with meat. Seasoning is essential to plant-based cooking.

Whatever doubts you may have about plant-based eating, the fact remains that most Americans are overfed and undernourished. A plant-based diet is rich in nutrients that have been shown to encourage healthy weight loss, help blood sugar and cholesterol achieve healthy levels, reduce inflammation, and protect against heart disease, stroke, and various types of cancer. With the possible exceptions of vitamin B-12 and vitamin D, which you can supplement as needed, your nutritional needs can be easily met with a plant-based diet. Any concerns you have about missing nutrients can be addressed by asking your doctor to test for deficiencies, but switching to a plant-based diet is almost guaranteed to increase the nutrients you take in each day.

Ethical vegans avoid animal products for moral reasons. They often choose to give up all animal food products, including honey, as well as anything else derived from animals, like leather. That's not my journey, and in fact, I still take honey in my tea and like to wear my favorite leather jacket, so I often avoid the word "vegan" to describe the way I eat and live. But the term "plant-based" can also be confusing. For some people, plant-based means no meat. For others, it means they still eat animal products but try to fill more of their plates with fruits and vegetables. To be clear, I don't consume animal flesh, dairy, eggs, or other animal products, with the exception of honey.

These days, I'm not a part-time plant eater. It's not a diet for me in the way we usually talk about diets as something we suffer through to look good for an event or until we can get off those last twenty pounds. This is the way I eat, and I no longer make exceptions for dessert or for anything else. I eat a vegetable-based diet with some fruit and grains. During summer, when so much fresh produce is in season and readily available, I mostly eat raw fruits and vegetables. I travel all over the world, and regardless of where I am, I manage to maintain this choice because I believe there's always a way. If that means I live off of rice and veggies for a week, that's fine with me.

For years, I bounced between thinking it was too hard, and thinking it might be hard, but I could make the switch to plant-based eating. Finally, I stopped letting myself make excuses and find exceptions. I decided I was taking this path regardless of what was going on around me. The Latin root of "decide" is *dēcīdere*, meaning "to cut off." I cut off all other options. There was no going back to my old way of eating. This is the power of choice and how we can take control of our lives. This is how we step out of the boat of physical mediocrity and walk on water.

While you do have to decide and commit, you don't have to give up all animal products at once. You can transition, one step at a time, like I did. I had already given up pork and red meat, but I read *How to Eat to Live*, by Elijah Muhammad, as a junior in college, and I immediately stopped eating chicken and turkey and limited my animal consumption to fish. Later, I watched the documentary *Super Size Me* and gave up fast food because the message of that movie came at the right time for me. After giving up meat that came from animals with legs, I was essentially a pescatarian, still eating seafood and dairy for years. My diet moved closer to a whole-food, plant-based diet over time before I completely made the transition.

Set a clear schedule for how you'll transition to plant-based eating. For the first month, choose one day a week to eat only plant foods. Month after month, add another plant-based-eating day to your week. A gradual transition will ensure you don't feel deprived by the change. At the same time, it will give you time to discover plant-based dishes you love.

Another option is to do what I did, but do it faster. Start by giving up pork and other red meat. Thirty or sixty days later, take chicken and turkey off the menu. After another month or two, cut out the seafood. Finally, in the last part of your transition, let go of dairy, including milk, cheese, the cream that goes in your coffee, and yes, those conventional desserts. Minimize the packaged foods you consume and read the labels. There are often hidden animal products in foods you would expect to be vegan-friendly, and replacing conventional junk food with vegan junk food is not a win.

What you include in a plant-based diet is just as important as what you avoid. There are plenty of unhealthy and overweight vegans who live off processed foods. White flour is vegan, but you don't want to live off the stuff. Processed sugar is vegan. Almost any conventional junk food can be found in vegan form. Food manufactures want your vegan dollars too, and they're slapping a vegan label on whatever they can. Fake butter, pastries, chips, candy, cookies—they might be vegan, but they don't deserve a regular place on your table. The majority of your food choices should still be recognizable as the living plants they came from.

Find recipes for vegan (plant-based) versions of your favorite dishes so you can still enjoy foods you love. Especially in the beginning, rely on beans, mushrooms, tofu, and meat substitutes to replace meat and give you that sense that you're eating something substantial. A plain chicken breast has very little flavor on its own, and just like you have to season your meat, you absolutely must season your vegan dishes if you want to enjoy your food. Keep your kitchen cabinet stocked with a wide variety of seasonings and spice blends, and experiment to find out what you like best.

A well-stocked kitchen will keep you from reaching for unhealthy options when you're hungry. Keep your pantry filled with brown rice, tortillas, whole-grain bread, nut butters, seeds and nuts, quinoa, beans, oatmeal, dried fruit, coconut and olive oils, and vegetable stock. Fill your refrigerator and freezer with basic salad ingredients, fresh fruits and vegetables, and the frozen fruits and vegetables you enjoy. Be willing to try new foods, even the ones you haven't liked in the past, so you can continue to expand your options. Invest in a high-speed blender to make quick soups and smoothies, and consider purchasing a juicer to make green juices.

If you're worried that you'll miss dairy, you have plenty of options. There are better plant-based cheeses on the market all the time. Nut-based cheeses are especially good, and if you're a cheese lover like I was, you'll want to try a few until you find one that satisfies your craving. There are also all kinds of plant-based milks and creamers, including almond milk and coconut milk, available in major grocery store chains.

Eating out and sticking to a plant-based diet can be challenging until you figure out how to work the menu. In most restaurants, you'll have to speak up and ask questions about how the food is prepared. In some places, beans for example, are cooked with pork. Whenever you can, choose a restaurant that has clearly identified vegan options on the menu. That's the best-case scenario, but when that's not possible, salads and side dishes are usually your best choices. Unless vegan dishes are marked on the menu, you'll have to interrogate the server a bit. The odds are you won't be the first person to ask about the ingredients in a dish, so don't be timid about questioning what's in the food you're paying to eat.

You might be surprised by how many vegetable dishes are flavored with meat, cooked with lard, or drizzled with butter. Be as clear as you can about what's in your food. One of the safest choices is to order rice and steamed or grilled vegetables. That combo got me through a trip to Ghana, even though many of the restaurant menus were meat-heavy and everyone around me was "vacation eating." If you're willing to make the effort, you can eat out and still eat plant-based.

As you transition to plant-based eating, expect some pushback from the people around you. Be ready for it, and don't allow other people to guilt or shame you into making poor choices. Your decision to take control of what you put in your body is yours to make, and you don't have to justify it to anyone. Explain as much or as little as you feel comfortable telling people about your decision to eat for health and longevity. Bring your own vegan dish to family meals with enough to share, or eat before you go. Some people will take your new way of eating personally, as if it were an indictment of their bad eating habits. Others simply have an emotional attachment to that macaroni and cheese Grandma used to make, and they'll feel threatened by the idea of a menu that would exclude their favorite dish. You don't need to prove anything or try to convince anyone to change with you, especially when you're in the early stages of your own transition. Care enough about your own health to stay focused regardless of how other people feel or what they say. You're making this change for you.

One of the best ways to honor your commitment to plant-based eating is to surround yourself with like-minded or open-minded people. Even if it means giving up some of what you're comfortable with, find your plant-based community. When I made the switch in how I eat, I also switched gyms. My trainer at my old gym had served me well, but the culture no longer fit me. I wanted to be around people who cared about fitness but who built their bodies with fruits and veggies. I moved to a gym that had a significant number of plant-based eaters and a culture that embraced that style of eating.

Your family and friends may never change the way they eat, but you can find a group of people who understand what you're doing and why. Especially in the beginning, this support will make it a lot easier for you to stick to your decision to live on the healthiest foods. Even if it seems like no one in your town could possibly choose to eat this way, there's usually a health food store, gym, or studio that has a small vegan community. If not, you always have the internet. There are vegan social media groups, sites, blogs, and forums, where you can get all the support you need.

You'll also need to set boundaries for your home. I like to entertain, but I maintain a plant-based household. If you come to dinner at my house, you don't need to bring a thing. I will feed you, and it will be a delicious plant-based meal because the days when girl's night meant a beautiful cheeseboard are over for me. Now, my friends know that, while you're in my home, you have to level up to my way of life. Decide what's acceptable in your home, and make sure your boundaries support you in your health goals.

FOOD, FAT, AND LOVE

Many of us hold on to food products that cause us harm because they also provide us with comfort. We silence ourselves through food. You can have all the right foods at home, a clear plan on how you will prepare them, and a sincere desire to eat for longevity, but you have a fight with your significant other, and before you know it, you're driving through the nearest fast food place ordering an extra-super-value-plus-combo meal. Your boss makes you stay late for work, and your kid is angry because you missed his game, so what do you do? You go to your favorite hamburger spot and order a double burger with cheese—and don't forget the fries and milkshake. You open the mail only to discover an unexpected bill, and instead of making the quinoa bowl you planned to have for dinner, you order a large pizza covered in sausage and cheese and eat the whole thing by yourself.

Understand that overeating, especially foods high in sugar, processed flour, and unhealthy combinations of carbohydrates and fats is typically a form of self-silencing. At the root of many poor food choices is a desire to avoid feeling uncomfortable emotions like pain, frustration, disappointment, or anger. We use food to sedate ourselves and hide from the realities of our lives. We self-silence with fries, and ice cream, and lasagna.

When you remove the foods you've used to tamp down your emotions, you can expect those emotions to rise to the surface and demand to be acknowledged. Be careful not to allow another substance or distraction to take the place of eating as a means of ignoring your feelings and desires. Replacing junk foods with binge watching, drinking, or compulsive shopping won't get you closer to the life you want to live. Be okay with feeling your emotions, and when you need it, get help from a professional to process it all.

Look at eating a plant-based diet as a way of loving yourself into wellness. Treat yourself with kindness as you transition to health. Give yourself room to make mistakes and get right back to your plan without beating yourself up. Learn how to accept the full range of human emotions and know that you're capable of managing them all. Find an outlet for your feelings. Talk with a therapist or pour your thoughts into a journal. Take away the power food has as a substance to be abused, and put it in its rightful place as enjoyable nourishment for your best body.

WE NEED TO TALK ABOUT ALCOHOL

While food is by far the biggest issue affecting our physical health, we can't skip over the issue of alcohol. Have you ever sipped alcohol out of a coffee mug or a to-go cup with a lid so no one would know you were drinking? Have you ever picked up a bottle of wine to pour yourself another glass, only to realize you'd already finished the entire bottle? Have you ever felt like an event wasn't worth attending unless there was an open bar? Have you ever left an event to buy your own alcohol since your hosts didn't provide any?

I've done all of that. I went through a phase during which I drank all throughout the day. My social plans were built around going out for mimosas in the morning and cocktails at night. God must have had his hand on my life because there were mornings when I woke up and couldn't remember driving home the previous night. One summer day, I spent the afternoon partying and drinking with friends on

Lake Lanier. We took a limo to dinner, where we had more drinks, and then I picked up my car to drive home. At first, like every drunk driver, I thought I was fine. But then my head bobbed, and the car swerved. I found myself struggling to stay focused and trying to convince myself I could make it home. I hit God with that prayer we say in moments of desperation. "God if you get me through this one last time," I prayed, "I promise I'll never drive drunk again."

When I woke up the next morning, one thing was clear. Drinking and driving just was not worth the risk. I could've killed myself or someone else. It happens every day, and I had been lucky it didn't happen to me. I imagined the shame and the guilt of taking someone's life because I was drunk behind the wheel. I imagined the hurt and embarrassment my family would suffer because of my bad choice. I imagined the terror felt by the victim and the pain and loss felt by the victim's family. I didn't want to be the cause of that kind of destruction. I would never drive under the influence of alcohol again.

There are defining crossroads in your life. At first, God throws a pebble at you, a gentle way of getting your attention. If you don't choose the right path, he tosses something a little heavier your way, say a rock. You can't miss it, but you still have the freedom to choose. If you once again choose the wrong path, he'll just keep tossing bigger, heavier, more painful attention-getters your way. A brick, maybe a boulder. That night was no more than a good-sized rock in my life. I didn't want to wait for a car wreck or a DUI arrest to finally make a much-needed change.

We silence ourselves with food, and we silence ourselves with drink. Alcohol, especially wine, is a mind-altering substance that has a cultural stamp of approval. Too often, we pretend it's a celebratory drink or just a little something to help us relax. Meanwhile, we use it to hide from our feelings, pretend we don't hurt, fake our happiness, and give boring or difficult moments an illusion of fun. It's so acceptable to abuse alcohol that we've come to think an occasion isn't really an occasion unless there's booze involved. While we're pouring all of those drinks, we're oblivious to the fact alcohol consumption can negatively impact fertility and damage our organs, trigger or aggravate depression and anxiety, dull our mental agility, and alter our mood so we're more likely to have relationship problems and less likely to feel motivated to pursue our goals.

You, me, all of us—we've been sold a bag of tricks about alcohol. You see lots of public service announcements and print ads warning people about the dangers of cigarettes, but with the exception of campaigns to prevent drunk driving, alcohol is still celebrated. TV doctors proclaim the benefits of red wine. Everyone you see having fun has a glass of something alcoholic in their hand. You can't advertise cigarettes on television, but alcohol commercials make it look like the only way to be grown and sexy is to drink beer, wine, vodka, or brown liquor. All the cool kids are doing it. Alcohol is a multibillion-dollar industry in the United States, and the marketing machine behind those sales has most people convinced that it's normal, sophisticated, and fun to drink as much as you want. We believe the message that the best way to relax after a long hard day at work or running behind the kids is to open a bottle of wine.

Many women get caught in a never-ending coffee–wine–coffee–wine cycle. We need wine to get to sleep at night, and then in the morning, we need coffee to jolt us awake so we can function. When I was drinking heavily, I was addicted to coffee. I had grown up drinking the stuff, and as an adult, I'd go to a coffee shop and order a triple espresso in the morning and go back for a double espresso in the afternoon. All the baristas at the local Starbucks knew me by name. While you can debate the nutritional merits of black coffee, the cream and sugar most of us add to the cup only serve to keep us further away from the excellent health we desire. I don't like being dependent on any substance, and when I stopped sedating myself with alcohol, I was also able to release coffee. I no longer needed caffeine to get me through the day.

Alcohol is full of empty calories, and it's a significant factor in the obesity epidemic. Alcohol misuse or abuse can also have serious detrimental effects on your overall health. Multiple studies have linked alcohol consumption to increased risks of cancer, including breast cancer. Alcohol prevents your body from absorbing necessary nutrients. It negatively impacts fertility, and chronic alcohol use can lower your immune system, disrupt digestion, and damage your heart, liver, and brain. It can cause your bones to thin and increase your risk of developing osteoporosis. If your overall health and longevity aren't enough to make you cut back on alcohol, then consider the way it affects your looks. Alcohol contributes to premature aging, including dry skin, puffy eyes, wrinkles, and broken capillaries.

For just over a year, I didn't drink at all. I wanted to eliminate the habit of feeling like I needed to drink. Now, I'll occasionally have a drink or two, but my days of depending on alcohol to have fun or to cope with life are over. If drinking alcohol has become a habit in your life, you're not weak. You're normal. Fortunately, it's a habit that you can break.

Decide what place alcohol has in your life. If you have a serious addiction, get help to stop drinking. If, like millions of other women, you've used alcohol to dull the ordinary pains of life, give yourself a chance to feel again. I'm not here to tell you to never have another drink. However, as a conscious eater, you need to be fully aware of the ways in which alcohol impacts your body, mind, and spirit. When you choose the action, you choose the consequence.

When you choose the action, you choose the consequence.

GET IN FIGHTING SHAPE

I'm a great admirer of champion athletes, including the world's best boxers. Seeing them in motion, you realize they have explosive power and strength. This has nothing to do with how heavy they can lift or how big they are. That greatness comes from within. It takes guts to get in the ring and fight, and even more once you've been hurt or knocked down. To get up and keep going is so much more than a set of skills. Heart is made up of a set of wills. You must have an inner belief in yourself, and a desire to win at all cost. If you truly want to get your breakthrough, you'll have to get in fighting shape, and it will require you to dig deeper than most people can and go where others cannot.

In one of the most iconic scenes in movie history, Rocky delivers an inspiring monologue to his son. He says, "You, me, or nobody is gonna hit as hard as life, but it ain't about how hard you hit. It's about how hard you can get hit and keep moving forward. That's how winning is done." Getting in fighting shape isn't going to be easy, but let's be clear: there is no easy path to victory. Greatness is a set of small things done day after day, workout after workout, time and time again. If you do not have a winning mindset, intense focus, and next-level work ethic, you may as well pack it up and go home right now. Everything you do or don't do is a choice. Whether or not you get in the best shape of your life will be up to you.

Anybody who knows me or has followed me on social media knows I go hard in the gym. Sweating is a stress reliever for me. I enjoy those hard workouts, and even in those moments when my body is completely spent and sore and ready to give out, I know I've accomplished something, and I can look forward to seeing and feeling the results. But I also know everybody isn't like me. I can't expect everyone to take the approach I take to exercise.

My basic exercise philosophy can be summed up in four words: *Move your damn body.* There's a little bit of "the warden" in me coming out in that sentiment, but that's really what it boils down to. Find something you like to do. Abs are absolutely made in the kitchen. You can't out-train a bad diet, but movement is essential to your overall health. The human body was designed to move, and if you try a variety of different activities, you'll eventually find something you like to do. Maybe it's walking or jogging. If you like to dance, then find a dance class. If you like the energy of working out with other people, find a group workout or boot camp that works for you.

If you've never been much of an athlete, don't let that excuse stop you. I was absolutely not an athlete growing up. In fact, I was a sickly and highly medicated child who led a mostly sedentary life. I suffered from allergies and severe asthma. At breakfast, I would break open a capsule of asthma medicine, sprinkle it over my grits along with plenty of sugar, and not think twice about it. I was that kid in class who always had her inhaler. At that time, the conventional advice for children with asthma was to keep us calm and still so we wouldn't have an asthma attack. I got used to hearing my parents say, "Sit down. Don't do that." It wasn't because I was doing anything wrong. I just wasn't supposed to play like other kids. I became afraid to run or risk getting out of breath. I told myself I wasn't athletic because the message I received was that I could never be active. Sports were dangerous to my health.

Now, I'm in the best shape of my life. I work out almost every day, and I don't hold back in the gym. My workout routines are usually high intensity, and I have no problem jumping on a treadmill and sprinting. I haven't had an asthma attack in more than five years, and the last incident was completely unrelated to exercise.

Even if you don't consider yourself an athlete, know that you will either use your body or you will lose your body. If you leave your car sitting in the garage for two years, the next time you get in it, when you finally need it, the odds are that it won't start. If you sit at your desk all day, and leave work and sit in your car, and get home and sit on the couch in front of the TV, scrolling through your phone, your blood never gets a chance to really flow. Your heart never gets a chance to test its ability to pump faster and grow stronger. When you need your body to move, it's not going to respond. Our bodies are machines, just like cars. You have to rev the gas on a regular basis if you want to keep your engine in good working order. When you see a 1956 Mercedes Benz 300SL in pristine condition, you turn your head and watch it go down the road. That car didn't just get that way. It had to either be consistently maintained or lovingly restored, and so it is with your body.

In the era of the quick fix, it can seem like working out is a waste of time. But waist trainers and detox teas are the equivalent of painting your car because the engine's knocking. Do you ever wonder what's going on behind the scenes with the Instagram star selling you the latest get-abs-quick gadget? Maybe she actually eats well and works out. Maybe she also had liposuction, a tummy tuck, and breast and butt implants. Maybe she just knows how to dress to look slimmer and find her angles in the camera. One thing is for certain: *no one gets lasting results from quick fixes.* They look like the easiest available options, but you can't get truly healthy or fit without making healthy choices day after day. Don't fall for the gimmicks. You deserve to claim something more than a temporarily tiny waist as your standard for health.

To get into fighting shape, you don't need to become the skinniest woman in the room. You just need to start on your way to becoming the healthiest woman you can be so you can fulfill your purpose. You cannot let the extra weight—physical, emotional, or mental—slow you down on your journey. You don't have time to stop and fill prescriptions for diseases you can prevent or reverse simply by making better lifestyle choices. You can't let a lack of energy, caused by refusing to properly fuel and move your body, stand between you and your destiny.

You just need to start on your way to becoming the healthiest woman you can be so you can fulfill your purpose.

Make better choices today than you did yesterday and better choices tomorrow than you do today.

So many women don't realize that wellness is available to them and this is largely due to the fact that wellness has been put into a tiny box that most of us will never fit into. Rarely does true wellness wear a face like ours in the media. Wellness is typically young and rich. Beauty is portrayed in extremes, but I want you to know, no matter where you come from, what you look like, or how far you have to go, wellness is as available to you as it is to anyone else. Contrary to what you may have seen or been told, fitness is not the exclusive privilege of blonde women who bounce around on TV and social media. Wellness is not the exclusive right of the wealthy. True wellness is a reclaiming of your birthright as a healer. Heal your body with food, just as our ancestors healed the sick with herbs and spices, tinctures and potions. Maintain your fitness with movement, as our bodies were designed to move. Connect to your spirit and elevate your mind by choosing to nourish yourself at the highest possible level. Get fit for your divine assignment.

So many women put their bodies through hell to look like something they're not. They have injections and implants and surgery. They burn their scalps and obliterate their edges. All of the superficial changes that give them a temporary sense of being good enough result in lasting damage. At the same time, they're convinced that things they really can control are too difficult or not important enough. They pass off responsibility for their health and longevity to doctors and pharmaceutical companies because they don't know how to or aren't ready to make the effort, to take responsibility for this one body they get for a lifetime.

Exercise isn't just a tool for weight loss or a way to mold yourself to fit a specific image of beauty. It's an investment in your short-term and your long-term health. Without regular exercise, you can expect your bones and muscle to weaken and lose mass over time, but strength training can reverse some of that loss and help you maintain strong bones and muscles. Many people worry about lifestyle diseases because they run rampant in our families, but your DNA doesn't have to be your destiny. Exercise can help prevent common illnesses, like diabetes, high blood pressure, and high cholesterol. It reduces the risk of heart attack and stroke and positively impacts anxiety disorders and depression.

If you worry about losing your mental sharpness as you grow older, then you need to make exercise a regular part of your life. Over time, working out can improve your brain health, including your memory. A consistent exercise habit can improve your skin health, increase your energy levels, help you get better sleep, improve your ability to manage stress, and increase the brain chemicals that make you feel happy in the moment.

You have the ability to step into the fullness of your own greatness, but you can't depend on anyone else to do it for you. You have to get out of your own way. You have to examine what you've always believed you were capable of and be willing to embrace the possibility that you have more control over your health and longevity than you've ever imagined. You have to know that a banging body is meaningless if you don't love yourself. You have to take responsibility for what you put into your body and how you manage your weight. You have to recognize and honor the connections between your body, your mind, and your spirit. You have to stop blaming other people for how you're stuck and recognize that only when you step up and take ownership of your physical wellbeing will you be able to fully experience the life you deserve.

Affirmation

I TAKE 100% RESPONSIBILITY
FOR MY LIFE AND
EVERYTHING IN IT.

5 FIND THE DIVINITY WITHIN

THE EXPERIENCE OF THE BLACK church tradition runs deep within me. My religious upbringing was solid and thorough. In my youth, my religious growth and education were cultivated in Antioch Baptist Church, in Cleveland, Ohio, and the people, practices, and lessons of that institution shaped me as a young person. I learned classic hymns and the latest gospel songs. I recited the scriptures until I could quote chapter and verse and apply Biblical principles to almost any situation. I was also well educated in what religion said was right and wrong, what was sinful and what was holy, what was correct comportment and what was incorrect behavior for a young Christian lady. It was life as I learned it was supposed to be, and a part of me yearned to follow the requirements and proscriptions dictated by church leadership. I wanted to do religion right. I read the Bible and went to church regularly, and in many ways, I was a better person for having done so.

Antioch also gave me a sense of my responsibility to the world around me. The people there trained me in the importance of community, compassion, and commitment. Going to church on a regular basis taught me how to give, how to serve, how to lead, how to be a public speaker, and how to see beyond myself. I learned respect for my elders and my history. Church taught me important principles and laid a solid foundation for how I would live my life. These lessons came from the pulpit, but they also came from the people who made up the church: the goodhearted aunties and grandmothers, the educators, and the ladies of Delta Sigma Theta, Incorporated, who poured into me, directly or indirectly.

BUT WHERE IS GOD?

Eventually, as I grew up, my religion was no longer dictated by my mother or my home church. As I left Ohio behind and made my own way in the world, I tried to keep up with what I'd been raised to do. In each new city, I looked for a church to join. I continued to study God's Word, and even though I was no saint, I endeavored to apply what I learned to the way I lived. However, as I approached my thirtieth birthday, I began to feel more and more like something was missing from my spiritual practice. God felt distant, so far away from me and my daily life. Even though I continued to go through the motions of religion, my spirit felt depleted and alone.

Around this time, I started drinking often and a lot. Alcohol became part of my lifestyle, and it took me some time to figure out I was using a substance, which temporarily numbed my emotions and silenced my thoughts, to try to find some peace, some joy, and some balance in my life. I used sex the same way, hoping a few moments of physical pleasure would ease the depression, fill the void, and make the pains of life's heartbreaks go away. During that time, I didn't see sex as two souls coming together. I didn't value that part of it. In both sex and alcohol, I sought something neither could provide me and which they actually kept me from getting. Physical intimacy with men, cocktails, and wine, dulled my pain for a short while—the same way food had when I was younger—but they also prevented me from making the connection I needed to make with myself and with Spirit.

During the time that I was starting to struggle to find my place in religion, I was invited to be the guest speaker for a Palm Sunday service at a church in Alabama. It was the spring of 2010, and I considered the invitation to be quite an honor. As I prepared for the event, my mom told me more than once, "They might not let you speak from the pulpit, so don't be surprised." I understood her concern. Many churches still enforce antiquated religious prohibitions against women taking positions of leaderships. However, I was certain such prohibitions wouldn't apply in my case. After all, I thought, *I'm Brandi Harvey, and I'm an invited guest on one of the holiest days of the year.* I told myself that if the leadership of that church didn't want to hear from a woman standing at the pulpit, then I wouldn't be speaking there on such a significant day.

When I arrived at the church, the pastor greeted me with warmth and enthusiasm. "We're so excited to have you here today!" he said as I shook his hand. After a little small talk, he explained that, since I wouldn't be sitting next to him, one of his staff would show me where to sit until it was my time to address the congregation. The woman directed me to a front row pew. "You'll be seated here," she told me, "and you'll speak from the floor."

The smile dropped from my face, and I flushed with a mixture of embarrassment and anger. My mother had tried to warn me, but honestly, I was still shocked. At that time of my life, I was seriously contemplating enrolling in theology school so I could become a pastor. In fact, I was so sure that my calling to teach would be fulfilled through preaching that I'd started to tell people that was my path. This church leadership didn't know me. They only knew me by reputation, and my reputation had been strong enough to get me the gig. Yet, because I had been created in the body of a woman, I was deemed not worthy of standing on the pulpit.

I ignored the rebellious voice telling me to grab my bag and leave. Instead, I stayed for the service, and gave my talk as planned—from the floor. But as I spoke, beneath my words of spirituality, recitation of scripture, hands raised to heaven, and smiles of grace, I was one pissed-off woman. The situation was a reminder of how, through the creation of rules that have no basis in the words or actions of Jesus, many faiths that fall under the umbrella of Christianity have silenced women for centuries. They've relegated women to a lower class and removed all femininity from the church, as if womanhood somehow represents a threat. Even though the Bible says man and woman are made in the image and likeness of God, woman has been deemed less than man. What's godly about that?

The experience did nothing to bring me closer to my Creator in that moment. However, it was one of several that propelled me on my quest to understand where religion, an institution of man's creation, might have veered from God's intentions for us. Nothing I read in the Bible, when taken in its full context, would have me treated as less worthy simply because I'm a woman. Religion had been one of the pillars of my life, but I found religious leaders who claimed to follow him often taught concepts that seemed to contradict the words and actions of Jesus. In the end, I decided to give myself the opportunity to find the connection to God I so deeply craved.

A NEW PERSPECTIVE ON CHRISTIANITY

It soon became clear to me that theology school wasn't my path. What I was seeking wouldn't be found in graduate school classrooms, and the message I wanted to share wouldn't fit the traditional paradigm. While I continued to study the Bible, I focused on understanding the words and actions of Jesus and separating fact from the meaning other people ascribed to his life to suit their own purposes. Books like Eric Butterworth's *Discover the Power Within You,* and *The Untethered Soul*, by Michael A. Singer, fed my hunger to understand more about the truth behind the words of the

Bible, the example Jesus set, my relationship with God, and how I could achieve spiritual evolution and contentment.

As I delved into a deeper truth about Christianity, what I learned reshaped my view of the man called Jesus and the religion created to deify him. I challenged myself to remain open minded, test what I learned against the words of the Bible, and welcome the insights and wisdom I could glean from other faith traditions. This search for God changed the way I live my life. What I learned brought me closer to the Divine than I had ever been.

Most eye-opening to me was what I learned about the history of the creation of Christianity as a religion and how the institution had been made by man, not by Jesus. This was a key revelation for me. Jesus, I realized, never asked that we deify him. He never created a church or set himself at the head of a religion as our God. Roman Emperor Constantine I and the First Council of Nicaea decided that Christianity would recognize Jesus as the Son of God, eternal and equal to God in his divinity. Thus, the decision was made by men. I further discovered that Jesus said, "Follow me," but he never said, "Believe in me and worship me as your God." He never said exalt me. He came as a teacher—one of many great teachers—and an example for us to follow. He came to show us how to recognize our own divinity and live it out in our daily lives. It was a group of men who, of their own volition, deified Jesus and created Christianity.

While this new information might, in the context of traditional Christian teachings, cause some to doubt their faith, it actually strengthened mine. It opened my heart and mind to possibilities I'd never considered. Through the example of

Jesus's life, we see that to truly give honor and praise to the Most High, we need quiet, prayer, and solitude. We see how he called us to prioritize love for our fellow human beings. We observe that he moved just as easily among society's lowest strata as he did among the elite, never leaving anyone behind. We see how we should strive to live our lives. I realized we all have so much more potential than we think we have, the same kind of potential Jesus had and fulfilled. It was a beautiful, compelling revelation for me, and it would forever alter my view of organized religion. While I still appreciate its value, I also recognize its limitations and its potential to limit us and our relationship with God.

SPIRITUAL OR RELIGIOUS

While I never felt a need to throw out the beauty and richness of the religion I grew up with, I started to question some of the beliefs I'd held for most of my life. As I began to challenge my own philosophies, I noticed other people my age doing the same. While many people before us had surely asked similar questions, I wondered if millennials as a group were moving away from their parents' religions and forging their own spiritual journeys in higher numbers. During this time, an unexpected opportunity fell into my lap, and it would enable me to dive deeper into answering that question—to take a journey, literally and figuratively, in my quest for spiritual realignment.

On Easter Sunday of 2014, my friend Lauren sent me the link to the website for a remarkable program and suggested

I apply. The Millennial Trains Project (MTP) is a non-profit organization that leads crowd-funded transcontinental train journeys in which young entrepreneurs and change-makers are given an opportunity to explore America's last remaining frontiers, those of social change. The premise is that the journey across the country (via train) and the meeting of like-minded voyagers and significant people at each stop will nurture leaders who will go on to tackle issues of social change and have a positive impact on local communities, our nation, and the world. It sounded great. I wanted to go. It was a perfect fit for where I was in my life at that moment. But there was a catch: I didn't have a research topic to propose. Lauren encouraged me to come up with something—any-thing—and submit my application.

Each participant was required to choose a unique area of study, and I decided the current state of religion and spiritual-ity in our country would be my focus. Anecdotally, I knew a lot of young people were seeking something more than what they'd found in the churches of their upbringing. They were seeking deeper connections with God, with other people, and with themselves. I typed up my proposal, pressed send, and a few weeks later, was accepted into the project. That summer, I packed my bags and boarded the train.

I'm forever grateful to Lauren for thinking of me when she heard about the program. My time on the Millennial Trains Project opened my eyes in new and unexpected ways. Riding in vintage passenger cars, we traveled across the northern part of our nation, and I had the opportunity to explore places I'd never seen. At each stop, we were treated to locally sourced food, and we met with city officials, influencers, and social innovation experts. The natural beauty of the region enchanted me, and the diversity of religions I was able to explore fascinated me.

In each city, I set out to better understand a spiritual practice different from my own. In Portland, Oregon, I visited the Grotto, a Catholic shrine. In Seattle, I visited a Buddhist temple, set up in a house in a residential neighborhood. I met with scientologists and with a psychic medium. My final stop was an audience with Queen Afua, at the Queen Afua Wellness Center, in Bedford-Stuyvesant, Brooklyn.

During our long rides from city to city, I had plenty of time to process all that I'd experienced and to meditate on what I'd learned. I also took advantage of the opportunity to share ideas with my cohorts. The Millennial Trains Project participants were a diverse group. They included Fulbright Scholars, a black atheist, Catholics, and people with roots in Korea, Yemen, Russia, Croatia, and Indonesia. Being in their company and talking with them afforded me the opportunity to really understand the roles religion and spirituality played in their lives, especially as they were growing up. As we talked, a common theme surfaced among my companions raised in organized religions with regular church attendance. It was the ever-present threat of hell and the need to follow a seemingly endless list of rules to avoid being sent there.

Their experiences echoed my own. My father was raised in the Church of God in Christ and my mother was a traditional Baptist. For them, everything was about following the rules. We couldn't wear pants to church, and even into my twenties, when I first felt called to evangelize, I would carry a lap cloth to church. Once seated, I'd lay the beautiful print scarf across my lap so my legs wouldn't show beneath the hem of my skirt. Like so many other religions' rules, modesty of that kind was ingrained in me.

The Millennial Trains Project was a watershed event in my life. Ultimately, I discovered that we all have more in common than I'd ever imagined. We all have an innate need to feel and give love. We all long to be treated with respect, honor, and dignity. Simply put, we are more alike than we are different. I became open to learning about and understanding other religions without judgment. I had always been a seeker, but I was looking at other religions and spiritual practices from a new perspective. I also learned to separate spirituality from religion.

Religion, I realized, is a construct of man, a framework that can be used for good or for bad, an institution that has contributed and caused harm. Spirituality is a connection with God and all of Creation, which can never be used for evil. By the time I disembarked from our last train ride, my hunger for spiritual growth and intellectual comprehension had grown. I now had more questions and a deeper curiosity. But I also felt richer and more empowered than ever to create my own spiritual life.

In college, I had dated a member of the Nation of Islam, and I'd even considered converting. However, as I studied the religion, I discovered it was even more rule-based than the church I belonged to, and I quickly decided I didn't want to trade one set of restrictions and prohibitions for another. At the same time, I struggled to reconcile my belief in a God of love with the idea that the gentleman I was dating was doomed to hell because he chose to be a follower of Islam rather than devote his life to Christ. He lived from a place of goodness in quiet, simple ways that had such a positive impact on everyone he interacted with in his daily life. How was it possible that he would never see heaven but anyone who was "washed in the blood" had every sinful thing they'd done forgiven? Finally, I began to understand that, with all the good I'd gotten from Christianity, religion had included many man-dictated rules that I didn't have to accept as a part of my life.

CHRIST CONSCIOUSNESS

Imagine living your whole life, from your earliest memory, wearing blinders, your feet shackled, your hands tied to your waist by chains. Then one day, someone comes along and unlocks the chains and removes the blinders. For the first time, you can stride or skip or run. For the first time, you can use your hands to create or to offer comfort. For the first time, you can see all the world has to offer you. Imagine the new sense of freedom and discovery as you take your first unrestricted steps and explore without restrictions or limitations. Simply embracing another person or watching a child play a game of her own creation and sitting down to join her would seem like miracles. Imagine how excited and inspired you'd feel about each new opportunity to use your new potential.

Most of us, to one extent or another, move through life chained and blinded by the limitations of our own beliefs. For too long, I lived my life that way. Because I believed

God was somewhere "out there" I searched for my Source outside of myself. Not until I challenged my beliefs about my relationship with God did I discover the truth of Jesus's greatest lessons. The kingdom of heaven was within me—as it is within all of us. To find and connect with God, I needed to stop going out and go within. As I glimpsed moments of Christ consciousness in myself and in others, something shifted inside of me. The void was starting to fill.

The person we call Jesus Christ was a man who discovered his own divinity and achieved true enlightenment in his unity with God. He showed us what it really means to be created in God's image. His oneness with God the Creator was meant as an example for us all to follow. The miracles he worked reflect how we can tap into our divine potential. They reveal to us our capacity to do great works when we act in one accord with God. Jesus wanted us to fully explore the power of our spiritual connection with God and all that makes us capable of becoming and accomplishing. When we are in harmony with the Creator, we can indeed perform miracles.

Christ consciousness is a recognition of the Christ-like divinity in you and in everyone else. It's an awareness of your higher self and a desire to choose to act from that part of you more and more often. It's a choice to follow the teachings of Jesus, not in a religious sense, but in how he lived his life every day. Discipline is one of the fruits of the spirit, and you can tap into a Christ consciousness through the spiritual discipline of your choosing—prayer, meditation, dance, yoga, silence, gratitude, reading holy texts—and through each choice you make throughout every day of your life. An openness to hear from God and a willingness to surrender beliefs and behaviors that do not serve that purpose is the first step to connecting to your higher self.

The spiritual walk is an inward journey. It's a walk you have to take alone. You can memorize verses and learn all the religious clichés, but without a connection to God, and this includes the God in you, something will always be missing. This journey does not require the attainment of perfection. It's the cultivating of your higher self, the part of every human being that's able to overcome and transcend our carnal instincts. Even the food I eat is a part of my spiritual discipline. I eat what tastes good and looks good but also makes me feel good and gives me the health and energy required to fulfill my purpose. Exercise is a spiritual discipline. I want to honor this temple God gave me by doing all I can to keep it in optimal condition. Treating people with kindness, honoring my word, acting with integrity—these are all spiritual disciplines and all a part of developing a Christ consciousness.

Even though I grew up under the religious teaching that sex outside of marriage was sinful and prohibited, a part of me started to discount that idea when I went away to college. It seemed like everyone around me, including the people who had similarly restrictive religious upbringings, was having sex. At nineteen years old, I looked around campus and felt like I might be the last living virgin. I wasn't so holy that I was saving myself. I was, in fact, looking for the right opportunity. I never thought abstinence would serve as a spiritual discipline for me, but I've discovered that it does.

I didn't decide to abstain from sex in my thirties because I thought it was sinful. I reasoned that if I honor my body by the food I put into it and what I choose not to eat, how I strengthen and stretch, how I rest and restore, then I should also be at least as conscientious about with what man I'm willing to be intimate. I now see sex as just as much of a spiritual experience as it is a physical one. For me, physical intimacy should be a connecting of souls. It's not so much that I'm just looking for a husband. I'm looking for my life partner with whom I can build a future as we lift each other and nurture our highest selves.

A Christ consciousness frees you from using the blood of Jesus as a crutch. All too often, we as Christians proclaim we don't need things of the world because we have Jesus. Women have told me that, although they struggle with childhood trauma from abuse they suffered, they don't believe they need therapy because they're covered in the blood. But if it were true that all we needed was Jesus, then no one in the church would be overweight, suffering from lifestyle diseases, or abusing drugs to cope with their pain. No born-again Christian would be going through his fourth divorce or spending her way into bankruptcy. If taking Jesus into your heart was a cure-all, the members of the church wouldn't even need the church anymore. We exhibit a Christ consciousness when we're willing to do whatever is necessary to evolve to be more Christ-like. If that means submitting to therapy or rehab or coaching to become more of who God would have us to be, then we do it.

A Christ consciousness means we endeavor to do everything as if we are doing it for God. I discovered that anything I do with love and with excellence I can do for God. One day, I was forty minutes into a work out. My trainer, Dooley, was yelling at us in this way he has that's military-like, and encouraging, and soul-connecting all at once, and his encouragement and his demands sounded almost like praise. And even though the next set was only going to get harder and last longer, I closed my eyes, and got into the zone. "Do it for God," I told myself. With every movement, I raised the weight higher. I wanted to go higher still, and I did. I wanted to give God my all in that workout, and I want to give God my all in the way I relate to other people, in how I build my business, and in every decision I make and action I take. I recognize that I'm created in the image of a multifaceted, beautiful God. I want to do my very best to honor that with excellence in all things.

A Christ consciousness moves us to see the Christ—the anointed one chosen by God for a special purpose—not only in ourselves but in everyone around us, even and especially when the God in them is hidden behind behavior we'd rather not endure. It's a sense of compassion and understanding for each person you meet on the street and where they are in their journey. It's forgiveness for the woman who took your spot in the group workout class or the man who cut you off on the highway. It's respect for the fact that we are all evolving at our own pace and in our own way. We must each run our own race, and there is no finish line we can cross to say we're done.

Jesus never taught religion. Instead, he represented our potential for oneness with the Divine. He showed us that, as we grow closer to God, we can be more and do more. However, it takes more than a walk down the aisle and a dip in the water to maximize that potential. For some people, the act of baptism, or similar religious rites, can be a beautiful public declaration of faith, and that's valuable. I've been baptized and would like to experience it again in my lifetime. A Christ consciousness, however, doesn't require anyone to become a Christian in the conventional sense of the word. It doesn't require ritual of any kind. Instead, you must wholeheartedly surrender your life. Followers of Christ must commit to become like Christ. By transforming our minds to achieve a Christ consciousness, we not only transform ourselves but also our world.

A REBIRTH: FREEDOM FROM ORIGINAL SIN

In John 3:3 (NLT) Jesus says, "I tell you the truth, unless you are born again, you cannot see the Kingdom of God." Accordingly, in Christian churches, we're taught the importance of accepting Jesus as your personal lord and savior. When you do, we say you've been "born again." That moment is usually symbolized with baptism, washing your sins away. However, I've come to see being born again differently. I now see it as the spiritual practice of surrendering. Just as Jesus had to submit to God, so too do we all need to submit and surrender our will, our ego, and our judgment. We are "transformed by the renewing of the mind," (Romans 12:2) but this transformation doesn't just instantaneously happen when you're dipped in the water. It doesn't happen because you confess a new faith of any kind. The renewing of your mind is a shedding of old beliefs, a surrender to God's will, and it's an ongoing process, a choice we make not once but again and again.

Through the renewing of my mind, I've released many of the beliefs, including religious beliefs, that I'd held for most of my life. At the core of this transformation was my rejection of the idea of original sin. So many churches lead with sin. We're taught that we were born of sin and it's a state we're doomed to live in, but that we must still fight against it for all of our lives. Too often religion becomes about living up to this impossible standard, leaving us forever crying out to God for forgiveness because we've once again fallen short. I no longer believe God is keeping a tally of our rights and wrongs, waiting anxiously to punish us if we step out of line.

Much of what has been tossed into the category of sin has been defined by man as such in order to get people to do what a particular society wants them to do. The threat of hell has for centuries been used to keep folks in line. True sin is when we choose our human nature over the divine nature we all have within us, but contrary to what many well-meaning religions teach, we are not inherently evil. When we choose evil, what we choose separates us from God. That is both the sin and the punishment. Separation from the Creator is a self-made hell.

> **Separation from the Creator is a self-made hell.**

Because we're made in God's image, we cannot be inherently evil. Instead, we have great potential for good. We have the power to create and to manifest. We have the power to perform miracles, to heal, and to teach. We have the power to create abundance. All that power, and for so many years, I'd failed to tap into mine because I didn't even know I had it. Now, I'm aware of my ability, and I've found ways to create peace and contentment without any of the coping mechanisms I used in the past. I challenged the belief that said my connection to God could only be made through Jesus, and in doing so, I freed myself to find infinite ways to make that connection.

I attend church when I'm moved to, but it's no longer an event or a requirement for me. It's an experience. I'm there not because I have to be, not because I'm afraid of what will happen if I miss a service, but because I choose to be there. I don't go to church because I think it's going to get me into heaven but because I long to renew my spirit or connect with a spiritual community. I want to learn something new and even have my own beliefs challenged. When I go to church, I expect more than great music and an engaging pastor. I expect to grow.

I don't go to a building to praise and worship every Sunday morning anymore, but that doesn't mean I've turned my back on church. I'm a member of a megachurch here in Atlanta, and I believe in the teachings of Jesus Christ. Through questioning my beliefs, I've come to know that. What I also know for sure is that I can connect with my Creator while I'm hiking in the hills, watching the sunlight dance among the trees, and listening to the birds call to one another. I can connect with God in quiet meditation, as the pen in my hand moves across the pages of my journal, or in the laughter of my beautiful young nephew. A spiritual experience requires us to be willing to change and grow. It requires us to challenge the beliefs that have been handed down to us and determine whether or not they still hold true for us.

Like most Christians and certainly most people who grew up in the traditional black church, I was raised to believe that there was only one way to get into heaven, only one way to be connected to God, only one correct path to follow. I no longer believe that. I refer often to the teachings of Jesus because he was one of the masters, but I believe God sent many great teachers who have given us Buddhism, Taoism, Islam, Judaism, and the other philosophies and religions that all lead to oneness with the Creator. I no longer judge one as better than the others. I challenged that belief, and it didn't hold up, and so I surrendered it.

When I was considering going back to school for a graduate degree in theology, I believed I was called to teach and guide people on their spiritual journey. Anyone who has ever heard me speak has heard the influence of church coming out of my mouth. With my speaking style and my study of the Bible, many people told me they thought I should become a preacher, and for a while, I thought so too. But I was brave enough to challenge that belief and change my mind. I still felt the same calling to teach in some way and to help people elevate their lives. I just needed to find a new way to fulfill it.

My study of other religious and spiritual belief systems, spiritual teachers, and experiences did nothing to diminish my love and admiration for Jesus and the way he lived his life. I haven't thrown out everything I learned from my religious upbringing either. What I got as a child, teen, and young adult from Antioch and other churches is still with me. You too get to choose what you keep and what you release from the religion of your upbringing. As an adult—a mature person—you get to decide who you are in your soul and what truth makes sense to you. I can't tell you what that is, but neither can the pastor standing on the pulpit. He is, after all, just a man. I believe that Jesus is one of several great teachers. I believe there are many paths to connect with Source. I believe that women and men are both created in God's image and endowed with great power.

If you have no particular spiritual beliefs, if you feel no connection to a Creator or you doubt one even exists, open yourself to possibility. Explore a wide variety of religions and spiritual practices and be willing to receive what they have to teach you. If, on the other hand, you're content with your beliefs in this area or so firm in your faith that this chapter has served only to annoy and anger you, remember that, as human beings, we're meant to be ever-evolving. What worked for your grandmother may not work for you. What served you well in your childhood may no longer be enough. Only you can recognize and decide what you choose to believe and practice. You will know you've found it when your spiritual life leaves you feeling fulfilled and connected to the Divine in all its many forms, including the divine in you.

You may question what you've been taught, what you grew up with, or what you currently believe and find you still think it's all one hundred percent on point. But you'll only have that confidence if you can be brave enough to ask the questions. I encourage you to challenge your beliefs as I did. Test them by studying your religious texts and others and learning about the history and background that influenced them. Put the words in the context of the time, place, and culture. Gain an understanding of what's been lost in translation.

I'm not trying to persuade you to believe as I do. Instead, I want you to no longer be willing to take things at face value. Standing on the pulpit or writing a book doesn't give anyone unquestionable authority. If you consider the Bible to be God's Word, then you can't afford to let other people interpret it for you. Those same words have been used to justify everything from genocide to slavery to denying women the right to vote. You have to understand the text for yourself by going beyond isolated verses and Bible stories. If you call yourself a Christian and that's your walk, then study the life of Jesus and seek to understand how he lived and what his life's mission truly was. Become a disciple of Jesus, and dive deep into his teachings. Allow yourself the luxury and privilege that many people will never have. Choose your own beliefs.

Affirmation

I AM ONE WITH THE CREATOR.

6 LIVE ON PURPOSE

WHEN I FIRST MOVED TO Atlanta, Georgia, I worked at a boutique, where I made eight dollars an hour. It was a survival job that allowed me to pay a few bills, but it certainly wasn't what I planned to do for the rest of my life. I felt dread and despair each time I drove there. I lasted less than two months, and I quit the very day I cast my vote for Barack Obama in the 2008 election. I refused to keep wasting my potential doing something that wasn't getting me any closer to my goals. The pain of working there and knowing I wasn't where I was supposed to be was pushing me toward my purpose.

In an interview on Oprah's *Super Soul Sunday*, Dr. Michael Beckwith, spiritual teacher and founder of the Agape International Spiritual Center, says that one of his favorite statements is "Pain pushes until the vision pulls."[8] That pain, that daily struggle, is the Universe pushing you towards your purpose. It will keep pushing you until you start choosing the right direction and allow your vision for your purpose to pull you. If you're thinking, "I don't have time to worry about my purpose. I'm trying to figure out how to keep the lights on and put gas in the car," you have not yet embraced the fullness of your potential. Once you understand that your potential is limitless because it comes from a God without limits, you will break out of survival mode and lean into your destiny.

You have all the power to change your life. There is no magic wand, but you can begin to activate your magical mind. You know you deserve more, but too often, your fear has made life more painful than it needs to be. That pain you feel is the imminent danger of living an unfulfilled life and settling for second best. Everyone has to experience some pain to give birth to their full potential, but understand the pain is not meant to be eternal. Stop playing it safe. The vision can pull you into your greatness if you will just allow it to do so. When you understand that your purpose is divinely placed, it will become too important for you to do anything but chase it down and make it a reality. The purpose you envision for your life may seem out of reach, but God wouldn't have given you a vision for it without also giving you a way to bring it to fruition.

In Matthew 14:22–33 (NIV), Jesus sends the disciples ahead of him while he goes to the mountain to be alone and pray. He has just performed a miracle, feeding the multitudes with two fish and five loaves of bread, and he needs to be one with God and get clear on his next assignment, and I imagine this was also a moment of deep gratitude for the miracle he had just performed. When Jesus finally goes to the disciples, they're in the boat, and the water is choppy. The boat, far from shore, is "buffeted by the waves." As the winds blow all around them, the disciples see a man crossing the water on foot as if he were on dry land, and they think it must be a ghost. Jesus essentially tells them, "It's all good. It's just me, Jesus," but Peter says, "Lord, if it's you, tell me to come to you on the water." It's as if he double-dog dares Jesus to prove his divinity, and Jesus says, "Come."

Peter wants an invitation, and Jesus offers it to him. When he steps out of the boat, when he steps out on faith, Peter also walks on water. He's afraid, but he does it. When Peter says yes to his divine invitation, he gets his breakthrough. Not until his faith falters does Peter begin to sink.

Your breakthrough is always going to show up in the form of an invitation, but you have to accept the invitation, get out of the boat of mediocrity, and walk on water. You have to step out on faith to step into your purpose. I can invite you to a conference or a retreat, but you have to say yes and show up to get your breakthrough. You have to do the work. The invitation to walk in your purpose is always there in some form or another. God has never rescinded your invitation to greatness, to power, to your destiny. Like Peter's, your invitation may show up in the middle of the storm, and you may be afraid, but when you get out of the boat, when you respond to that test of faith by affirming your belief in the power of God and the divinity God has placed in you, your breakthrough is imminent.

CHOOSING PURPOSE

Some of us will get ten years or less on Earth. Some of us will get one hundred years or more, but our time is always finite. Of course, we all know that on some level, but when we know but don't act on that knowledge, it seems we don't have a deep and clear understanding of it as fact. Once you really develop an awareness of your time, you change the way you use the hours of each day. You no longer have time to waste. You invest your hours in completing your assignment before the due date catches you short. When you truly understand that this life is going to end whether you do what you came here to do or not, your purpose becomes your driving force. Minister Myles Munroe called this having "an acute awareness of my time." When you have an acute awareness of your time, you move every day to act on your purpose and fulfill your assignment.

Your purpose is your divine assignment. It's why Spirit placed gifts in you that no one else has in the same quantity, quality, or combination. Your purpose is your why. It's the reason you're alive. It's the reason your spiritual being is having this human experience. It's not something you are. It's something you do. Like any assignment, your purpose requires you to take action to complete it. Florence Griffith Joyner had to train with passion, consistency, and discipline. Beyoncé has to practice with passion, consistency, and discipline. Venus and Serena Williams have to play tennis with passion, consistency, and discipline. Michelle Robinson Obama has to study and work with passion, consistency, and discipline. With the exception of Florence Griffith Joyner, whose mission is complete, these women continue to put in an exceptional amount of effort to live their purpose. That's a choice they have to make every day.

You don't have to be the nation's first lady to live your purpose. Be the first lady of your own life. You don't have to be a track star or a tennis champion. Be the champion of your purpose and the star of your story. Choose to go after your purpose with everything you've got.

YOU ARE NOT PURPOSED TO BE THE NEXT BEYONCÉ

Your purpose is unique to you. You can't find it by imitating someone else. Somewhere in the world right now, a little girl is in front of a full-length mirror, holding a hairbrush like a microphone and trying to move and sing like the greatest musical superstar of her time. This little girl might have a lovely voice, or she might not be able to carry a tune. Either way, she's not destined to become the next Beyoncé. The world already has one, and as good as she is at what she does, we don't need another one. That little girl singing in the mirror might turn out to be a musical genius, or she might discover that her purpose is to be the background singer who helps the next pop star shine. She might become a doctor or a computer programmer, a lab technician or a personal trainer, but if she does what she's destined to do, it won't be an imitation of anyone else.

Because our culture places such a high value on grabbing the spotlight, many people think they want to stand in front and hold the microphone whether they're purposed to it or not. But few people think about the hours Tina, Matthew, and Beyoncé Knowles put in to create the entertainer we know as Queen Bey. You don't get to be the queen without doing the work. Her parents recognized a gift in her and nurtured it to bring it to fruition, but they could only influence her in the direction of her purpose. Beyoncé had to keep the vision in front of her and stay focused on it. She had to travel the road for herself. What the next phase brings will be unique to her. That's her purpose, not yours. You are not purposed to be the next Beyoncé. You are designed to become the highest version of yourself.

Your purpose is not the same as anyone else's. It's fine to draw inspiration from other people, but you have to know you are uniquely designed and gifted. It can be scary to claim your purpose because, once you say it out loud, people might hold you responsible for living it. Sometimes it's easier to say you want to do something that seems impossible, something you know you're not created to do. After all, who's going to take you seriously when you run around saying you're going to be the next Oprah, the next Maya Angelou, or the next Michelle Obama? It's a way of protecting yourself from having to try because your failure is already assumed.

More common than declaring a lofty, out-of-reach purpose is the claim that you have no idea what your purpose might be. So many people say they don't know their purpose, but in reality, they're afraid to share what they believe they were created to do in this world. They're afraid it won't sound glamorous enough, good enough, or ambitious enough. Sometimes, they've pushed it away because they've been told in no uncertain terms that their purpose isn't worthy. But comparing your purpose to someone else's or measuring it by any standard other than your own is a trap. When you're busy watching someone else and wanting what they have or trying to find a purpose that will please and impress other people, you're wasting the time, energy, and resources you should be putting into the pursuit of your own unique purpose. Losing sight of your purpose is the price you pay when other voices drown out your own.

Imagine a little girl who loves to spend her days outside with the sun on her face and her hands in the soil. She says she wants to be a farmer, and people smile and pat her on the head. As she gets older, they tell her, "Oh, you don't really want to do that." Her classmates laugh at her ambition. Her school counselor tells her farming is a dying occupation and there's no money in it. She needs to find something more stable and dependable to do with her life, the counselor advises. All along the way, the little girl gets so much pushback that she eventually questions why she ever longed to work the land and grow food that would nourish people and bring them pleasure as they came together around the dinner table. She grows into a woman and gets a nice office job, something respectable that pays well. She plants a garden on the side of her house and shares her harvest with her neighbors. She lives a good life, but she's always haunted by a nagging sense of discontent.

Now, imagine the same little girl, happiest outside connecting with the land and helping plants grow. Her parents recognize her passion and buy her a set of child-size gardening tools. They cordon off a small plot in the yard where she plants cucumbers and strawberries, peppers and melons. Tending her garden isn't a chore for this little girl. She enjoys it. It comes easily to her. At school, she tells people she wants to be a farmer when she grows up, and while a few students giggle, her teacher tells her that's a very important job. Her school counselor suggests she consider agricultural school. The little girl grows into a woman who owns and manages an organic farm. She supplies seasonal produce to the local farmer's market and invites schoolchildren to tour her farm and learn about how their food grows. She goes on to develop new farming techniques that produce greater yields without adding dangerous chemicals to the food supply. She lives a good life, and she has the satisfaction that can only come from living your purpose.

Few people will have a journey to purpose as beautifully unobstructed as the second version of that little girl's story. Our parents are imperfect, and even when they're well intentioned, they often project their own biases on our life choices. As children, many of us have experiences with schools and teachers that are less than supportive of our individuality. When our sense of self-worth isn't as strong as it should be, we're likely to give in to the pressure and follow the crowd even when it comes to something as important as our purpose. But as you'll see, overcoming those obstacles often plays an important role in preparing us to fulfill our purpose. First though, you have to get clear about what your purpose is.

DEFINING YOUR PURPOSE

As a little girl, my twin sister, Karli, displayed a natural talent for hairstyling. She had a gift for it when we were as young as nine years old. When we went to the salon to get our hair done, the owner would let us play with the mannequin heads, and while I didn't have much patience for it, Karli was in her element. She did meticulous finger waves and roller sets on the mannequins, and it came easily to her. It was a gift. However, when she said she wanted to be a hairstylist when she grew up, our family rejected the idea. Our mom told Karli that, no, she wouldn't be a hairstylist. She was going to college.

Later, in our teenage years, Karli showed a talent for cooking. When we were fifteen, she won the church bake-off with a sour cream cake with fresh strawberries and homemade whipped cream. She came home with a set of kitchen tools and utensils that would've inspired any baker to get to work. Some parents would've seen the gift and passion my sister had for food and encouraged her to take a baking class or two, consider culinary school, and see how far she wanted to take it. Again, our mother steered Karli to a traditional four-year college program.

Our mother wasn't trying to squash Karli's talents. She was trying to protect her daughter and make sure Karli had the greatest possible chance to build a successful life. For our mother's generation, any profession that had a hint of physical labor was to be avoided. For too long, the option to go to college was closed to most black people. In the decades following the end of slavery, most of us were limited to domestic work or other manual labor that rarely scratched the surface of our talents or skills. My mother, like so many black parents of her time, wanted more for her children. She wanted us to have a profession that didn't require us to stand on our feet all day.

Karli went to a four-year college. She did enough to get by and graduate, but she had no real vision for her degree, and so, she had little enthusiasm for it. Not long after she finished school, she decided to attend the prestigious Vidal Sassoon Academy. Unlike when we were in college, she was never late for a class, she stayed late for every extra credit opportunity, and she went above and beyond in all of her work. Karli passed her exams on the first try. She thrived in cosmetology school because she was operating in her gift and following her purpose.

Today, my sister's hair is still always laid and her makeup flawless. Most days, she spends time creating healthy and delicious meals, beautiful dishes fit for a magazine cover. Whatever her future holds, you can be sure her purpose will allow her to express her gift for creativity. She knew that was her purpose from a young age, and she has the freedom now to define for herself how it will manifest.

If you can't clearly articulate your purpose today, you have a responsibility to rediscover it. You may have been dissuaded from it when you were a child. Maybe people laughed at you and said someone like you could never accomplish something like that. Maybe someone told you your purpose wasn't good enough. Or you may have gotten distracted from your purpose as the obligations of adulthood piled up in front of you, little by little, until you could no longer see what lies ahead on your journey. Whatever the case, the time is now to get clear about your purpose. Get out of the boat, and let the vision pull you in the direction of your purpose.

In the same 1990 sermon in which he speaks about "an acute awareness of time," Bishop Munroe explains the importance of understanding the purpose of anything. "If you don't know the purpose for something," he says, "you will abuse it."[9] He defines abuse as abnormal use and explains that when the purpose of a thing is not known, abuse is inevitable. So if you don't know and respect the purpose of a pain medication, you're likely to abuse it. The consequences of that are bad enough, but if the thing in question is your life, then you need to sit up and pay attention. If you do not know the purpose of your life, you will abuse it.

There is no doubt that God is a god of purpose. Proverbs 19:21 (NIV) says, "Many are the plans in a person's heart, but it is the Lord's purpose that prevails." God has a purpose for every one of us. You might resist it, but that doesn't change the fact that it's yours. Finding your purpose only becomes complicated when other voices drown out your own. It only becomes difficult when the noise we all live with drowns out the voice of God in you. Your purpose is born of the passion you have burning inside you. It's that gift God placed in you that allows you to do what you do better than anybody else. It's the natural result of that thing you could do in your sleep. It comes so easily to you that you might take it for granted, but your gift is at the root of your purpose. In order to fulfill your purpose, you have to show up and operate in your gift every day, in whatever way you can in your current circumstances.

If you're clear about your purpose, but you believe you just don't have the money, or the resources, or the connections to fulfill it, then you need to stop and examine this goal you're calling your purpose. God doesn't give you a purpose without giving you the provision and opportunities to make it happen. That doesn't mean it will happen overnight or that the journey will be easy, but God's abundance is available to you. If what you think is your purpose seems impossible to accomplish, then either it's not your purpose or you're using a scarcity mentality to avoid taking the risk and doing the work.

I knew from an early age that I was called to teach and lead. As a child, when I spoke in church and led prayer service, I was developing skills that would be essential to my purpose. I learned how to stand in front of an audience and hold their attention. I came up with plays, like our Easter play, "They Killed My Homie Jesus." Even though I was never going to be a soloist, I performed in show choir. Through theater and music, I cultivated my confidence and my stage presence. For a while, I fulfilled my purpose by managing an afterschool program, and by the time I graduated from college in 2005, I had a plan for how I would step into my role as a teacher. I imagined I'd spend three years in the classroom, get my doctorate, become an administrator, and finally wind up as a young school superintendent in a district where I could make a real difference. But I haven't taught in a classroom in over a decade, and I no longer desire to work for any school system. I had a plan, but God knew my purpose.

> God doesn't give you a purpose without giving you the provision and opportunities to make it happen

When I got heavily into fitness, I became a fitness instructor, so even in that world, I was teaching. Later, I went to work for my father's foundation. I was still able to serve and teach women as a small part of my job, but I had really gotten distracted from my purpose. I allowed my desire to be close to my father and to have him recognize and acknowledge me to derail me from what I was meant to do, and not surprisingly, it didn't end well. As I felt the foundation going in a direction that didn't align with my purpose, I could've made the decision to move on to something else. Instead, I held on because, in my mind, the job was intertwined with my relationship with the person whose approval, respect, and attention I craved most. To leave the job would mean leaving behind any chance of winning what I felt like I needed from my dad.

I didn't want to give up the job, but I was slowly letting it go. When decisions were made that I didn't agree with, I protested by doing things my way anyway. And if I couldn't do that, I went along begrudgingly. In the weeks that followed what I knew would be my last mentoring camp as the executive director of the foundation, I reached out to my dad to try to find some time to get together and talk. However, I still didn't acknowledge what was going on or offer my resignation. Eventually, I was fired.

Fortunately, I knew it was my time to follow my passion for teaching and leading women, and I entered a stage of intense learning and growth as I figured out exactly what my next step would be. But I also made an important shift. I started letting my vision pull me, so the pain no longer had to push me. Today, I'm living my purpose by writing this book, growing my active wellness brand, Beyond Her, and speaking to women and girls all over the globe. God's will for my life was bigger than any plan I had for myself. As I took more and more responsibility for my physical, mental, emotional, and spiritual wellbeing, my whole life began to elevate, and I became better able to execute on God's will. It's all connected. I became a better teacher by becoming a better me. Now, I have a clear vision for my purpose, but I remain open to hearing from Spirit about the direction I should take. I am always listening for a new invitation.

THE VALUE IS IN THE JOURNEY

While my time at the foundation did take me out of my purpose to some extent, the pain of the way that experience ended pushed me to make some important decisions for my life. I started seeing a therapist. I launched my own business. My focus on my vision sharpened. If I chose to look at that phase of my life as wasted time, then it would be exactly that. But when you look at your journey and figure out how to take what you've learned from your pain and your past and apply it to your purpose, that's when you see a true transformation.

Running my dad's foundation gave me a unique opportunity to strengthen the skills I'm using to run my own business today. When I was working in the fitness industry, I developed the discipline and consistency it takes to maintain a high level of fitness. That time in my life fueled my desire to understand the best way to eat and led me back to the plant-based eating I'd toyed with, off and on, for years. My experience with the Millennial Trains Project opened my mind so that I turned from doing church to pursuing a relationship with my God with fresh fervor. None of it was wasted. It was all a part of the journey. And it's all serving my purpose.

Every time I've been tested in my physical, mental, emotional, or spiritual life, I've grown and come out better prepared to live my purpose. Development in each of these areas was, and still is, necessary for me to perform at my highest level. The lessons I take from my journey make me a better daughter, sister, lover, friend, teacher, and business owner. When you're willing to look at your experience, learn from it, and do the work to grow in every area of your life, you cannot help but be transformed. You cannot help but be moved closer to the fulfillment of your purpose. When you're walking in your purpose, you can never look back on your life experience with regret because, no matter how far you believe you wandered from your path, as long as you return to your purpose, all things can be used for your good.

In his allegorical novel *The Alchemist*, author Paulo Coelho describes purpose as a Personal Legend, which can only be fulfilled by going on a journey and learning from your experiences on that journey. In the book, we see that we all have a destiny to fulfill, but it doesn't just happen to us, and our purpose is not just a single destination. Our transformation is predestined. It occurs during the journey through which we're constantly unfolding. Essentially, the journey—if you're willing to take it—and your purpose are inseparable. You cannot live out your purpose if you're not willing to take the journey that leads you there.

Michelle Obama was purposed to be this country's first lady. But she wasn't born walking, talking, looking, and thinking as a first lady. Even when Barack Obama started running for office, Michelle didn't look the same as she did after she got the title. The change we all saw in First Lady Michelle Obama was born of much more than just the additional resources and access she had once they were in the White House. That change came from all the work she'd done and knowledge she'd acquired along the way. She was ready for that change.

If you're not willing to take the journey, overcome the obstacles, and learn from the challenges, you will never achieve your purpose. You have to do the work. If a friend tells me God told her she's going to write a book and publish it by the end of the month, but she hasn't written the first page yet, I have to question whether or not she made that up in her own mind or she's simply choosing to ignore what Spirit is telling her to do. Because God can give you the vision, God can order your steps, but you've still got to pick up your feet. If God is telling you that your purpose is to be an author, you've got to start typing the pages. You have to get out of the boat and start walking on water.

At one point in time, I convinced myself that fitness was going to be my life's work. I thought I'd compete my way up to Ms. Olympia because I loved working out and what it did for my body. But the truth was that becoming the most sculpted woman in America was never my purpose. Fitness is just a part of my journey. Staying in peak condition keeps me mentally sharp and motivated to take action, but I'm not called by God to pose and flex and put my body on display for judging. I'm called to teach and lead. No matter how many times I step off that path, I'm pulled back to it, and I return to do the work of teaching and leading again.

While we all have a personal journey and a destiny to fulfill, and no two purposes are alike, every purpose is bigger than the person living it. Jesus came to teach us first and foremost about the love of God and how we can live out that love in our lives. He came to show us how to live with goodness, and mercy, and compassion, and grace. That's the kingdom he speaks of us building, not a kingdom in the sense of a religion but in the sense that we are each to fulfill our purpose from a place of love for God and for each other, from a place of appreciation and gratitude for the gifts God has given us. That's how we change generations. That's how we live out our ultimate purpose, by using our gifts to that end.

STEP INTO THE ARENA

When I worked as the executive director for the foundation, one of our sponsors was the United States Army. One year, the Army representative I worked with offered me a unique opportunity. I had a chance to skydive with the United States Army Parachute Team, also known as the Golden Knights. At first, I was a little reluctant. I had a desire to do it, but as the day drew closer, I wondered what I'd gotten myself into. Typically, my fun does not involve fear, but when I expressed some doubt, a lieutenant colonel told me how few people get that opportunity. She looked me in the eye and asked, one black woman to another, "How many of us do you think will get this chance?"

She was right. It was a once-in-a-lifetime opportunity, and I had to go through with it. I made the decision, but that didn't alleviate the fear. As we took off and the plane climbed higher and higher, I realized just how far up in the air I'd be. It was all too real as I watched the first two skydivers fall out of the plane much faster than I'd expected. I was tandem-jumping with one of the best skydivers in the Army, one of the best in the world, but as I looked down at the Earth and saw what looked like a Google map below, the real fear set in.

My skydiving partner counted, "One, two," and we jumped. And the intense fear took my breath away. I was falling fast when I remembered the photographer assigned to take pictures and videos of my jump. I tried to think of something to do for the camera, but I was so scared that the best I could do was to flash the peace sign.

But then the parachute opened. As we coasted over San Antonio, Texas, on a clear, sunny day, my tandem partner asked if I wanted to take off my goggles to see better. At first, I was too paralyzed with fear. "It's okay," he told me. "You're good."

He was right. I was good. I lifted my goggles and saw the world from a perspective few people will ever get to enjoy. I could hardly believe I'd done it.

Making a major change in your life requires you to take a leap of faith just like that. Your life might not be on the line the way mine was when I jumped from an airplane, but you risk failure. You risk embarrassment. You risk discomfort, and you risk alienating the people who are comfortable with you just the way you are. When you jump into your purpose, you don't know who or what might catch you, but God gives you grace when you have the guts to leap.

God gives you grace when you have the guts to leap.

Most people lose in their lives because they choose to be spectators. They sit in the stands and watch everybody else make moves. They're afraid to get the cuts and bruises, so they never get in the game. In his often-quoted 1910 speech now known as "The Man in the Arena," Theodore Roosevelt said, "It is not the critic who counts; not the man who points out how the strong man stumbles, or where the doer of deeds could have done them better. The credit belongs to the man who is actually in the arena, whose face is marred by dust and sweat and blood . . . and who at the worst, if he fails, at least fails while daring greatly, so that his place shall never be with those cold and timid souls who neither know victory nor defeat."[10]

In this life, if you want to get your breakthrough, you have to step into the arena and perform. The speaker on the stage may stutter, the athlete may stumble, the doctor may lose a patient or the attorney a case, the singer may hit a false note, and the politician may not get enough votes to win the election, but they're in the arena. They're the living proof that the people who make change in this world don't get through it unscathed. They're the people who walk in bloody and bruised and take the hits and keep going.

Starting something from the ground up takes courage. It takes guts to be creative, to create something that didn't exist before you put your hand to it, to put yourself out there. Out of the dirt, God formed Adam, and when you want to create, you too will have to get your hands dirty. You have to take the risk, even when it doesn't make sense to anyone else. You can't do it from the sidelines, from the stands, or from your couch. You have to step into the arena to fulfill your purpose.

When I was finally fired from the foundation, I was released to my destiny. I knew who I wanted to serve and the change I wanted to make, but I didn't know how that would manifest in reality. Launching Beyond Her helped me step into the arena of my life. When I write to my community, I'm writing from my heart. It takes guts for me to talk about going therapy as a black woman and the daughter of a megastar. It takes guts to show my humanness so I can reflect the layers of humanness in every woman. Each morning when I get up, each time I walk out the door, I get a chance to step into the arena, and I take it. I deliver. I perform. I give it my all.

Someone has been waiting thirty-six years for me to get my breakthrough so I can show her how to get her breakthrough. The moment you have your breakthrough, you give license to other women to make change in their lives. You give them a license to get therapy, to start a business, to write a book, to lose the weight, to heal themselves. And that takes power. That takes guts. That takes courage. You have to be brave. You might think nobody is watching you, but you're wrong. You have the ability to bless somebody when you show up in your own life. That's stepping into the arena. You have to trust God enough to lay it all on the line. No guts, no glory.

Many women think their highest calling is to give birth, and so they feel unfulfilled. They believe that, because they're not married or having children yet, they can't fulfill their purpose. But we're always in the birthing process. You may be meant to birth something other than a child. You may be meant to birth something in spirit form, a project that changes lives, a ministry, a program, a business, something to help humanity in a way far greater than you've imagined. You may be called to birth something that positively impacts generations.

THE POWER OF THE PAUSE

Every good public speaker, every trained actor, and every effective preacher understands the power of the pause. You've seen them use well-placed moments of silence in monologue or dialogue, and you've experienced that power. That little space allows the audience to intellectually and emotionally process what came before it. It allows people a chance to really hear. There's a similar power of the pause in the fulfilling of your purpose. There will be times in your journey when the best thing you can do is nothing. Not nothing in the sense of idleness, but nothing in the sense that you shut down, shut off, and shut up. That pause holds the space for you to hear your own voice, and in that silence, you cannot help but hear the voice of God.

So often, we want to make decisions by committee. We want to pursue our purpose, but we want our parents, our partner, and our friends to sign off on it first. We want agreement and consent to make us feel better about our choices and to have someone to share the blame if we don't get the results we expected. We want someone to walk our journey with us because a faulty belief system has us convinced that we can't walk it alone. But the truth is that alone is the only way you can take your journey and fulfill your purpose. Yes, you'll have help along the way. But your purpose is not your husband's purpose. Your sister and your children have their own purposes to realize. Sometimes, the best choice you can make is to stop trying to rope other people into your purpose and get still.

Ultimately, the only one who can complete your journey with you is Spirit. Our greatest spiritual teachers demonstrate this when they seek solitude in their moments of decision. Jesus used solitude as a tool to prepare for his work, to manage his emotions, to make life-altering decisions, and to commune with God. He didn't seek confirmation from the people around him. He went inward and away from the world. The fact is that your purpose is between you and your God, just as Jesus's was. No one else can confirm for you that the purpose you're pursuing is the right one. No one else needs to confirm it.

You will absolutely have moments when the only way to know which step to take next will be to shut out the noise and get quiet. You'll also have moments when it would be a whole lot easier to step into your purpose if you had someone to hold your hand and take that leap with you. But you'll have to find the courage to go alone. When the time came for him to take up the cross, Jesus didn't call out for someone to hold up the left side and someone else to hold up the right. In the moment of his greatest act, the moment in which he fulfilled his ultimate purpose, he carried his burden alone.

You don't have to wait for your defining moment to enjoy the unique gifts of solitude. When I decided to participate in the silent retreat, I was seeking the silence that would allow me to connect with my God. I wasn't alone in the physical sense, but without conversation, radio, internet, or television, I had a unique experience of solitude. My intention was to be present and to be open to revelation and breakthrough. I was imperfect in the process, breaking my silence when one of the other retreat attendees frustrated me with her behavior, but even that moment revealed something important to me. I discovered that we often use our words as a coping mechanism, in the same way that

In the moment of his greatest act, the moment in which he fulfilled his ultimate purpose, he carried his burden alone.

we use things like food and alcohol and the distraction of social media or television to silence our emotions. Everyday entertainments like music and reading can provide a buffer between us and our feelings. I had given up eating unhealthy foods and stopped drinking alcohol for a period of time, but with none of my other coping mechanisms or release valves to rely on, the first part of the retreat was difficult for me.

The thought that I could just go home at any time played on a loop in my head. Moment by moment, I had to make the choice to stay because going so deeply into silence required me to get uncomfortable. I was surrounded by people with whom I wouldn't necessarily have chosen to spend so much time. I snapped at a woman, breaking my silence because I didn't manage my emotions in that moment. I grew tired of the hours of yoga, and meditation, and activities that didn't always make sense to me. However, because I had set a clear intention to commit to the experience and encounter both God and myself during the retreat, I didn't leave, and there came a point when I broke through and found the beauty of the silence.

Here's an excerpt from my journal, written after three days of complete silence.

Saturday, October 28, 2017

It rained like hell today. It's as if you can see Heaven and Earth moving together in unison, on one accord. Simply beautiful. It's as if God was cleansing us, this last day in silence, washing away the old, clearing a path for the new, a proverbial baptism, but in a spiritual sense. Not take me to the water, but rather cleanse every step, wash away my old life today, and clear away the debris so that my new life can emerge. The silence made the path renewed. It removed the clutter, swept the floor. The rain mopped it, cleared it.

I sit outside of class today in the cold rain, just standing, soaking it all up. The crisp air, the trees, the leaves, the colors, the mountain. Oh my god, the mountain, the mountain! The mountain reminds me of how Jesus went to the mountains to pray, to seek a silence and solitude. The disciples went to the mountains. Martin Luther King Jr. went to the mountain. The mountain speaks to the solitude, the aloneness, oneness with the Creator.

It's as if you are standing at the epicenter of Heaven and Earth, and couple that meeting of Earth, sky, land, creation, with the ultimate Creation that God formed. It's as if you are standing ready for God to pour into you. But this morning, I stood looking out onto Heaven. Heaven right here on Earth, beauty and wonder and all things divine. I smile. I was so grateful, grateful for the decision to be faithful and follow the divine voice of God inside that told me to come here to Boone, North Carolina, to the mountains, to meditate in silence with people from around the world, from across the United States. I stood there thanking God, with so much gratitude in my heart, for allowing me to have my mountaintop experience. I was grateful this morning, to commune with the Creator, to bask in all of the beauty and splendor which makes life worth living.

I am leaving some old bags on this mountain. Things that no longer serve me and are too heavy to carry. Some old thoughts and ideas that are no longer needed to continue the rest of my journey. For the next chapter of my life, I say thank you, and you are welcome. Have thine way. Let thy will be done. And I believe that is my greatest takeaway from this week. Have thine own way. Let thy will be done, done in my life, and then the lives you want me to teach and touch, God.

I leave ego and selfishness on this mountain. I leave fear and regret on this mountain. I leave the feeling and need to have opinions and approval of others. I am divine. I am the manifestation of the Creator made with care and love, with a keen attention to detail. I leave low self-esteem on this mountain. This experience has made me far more beautiful. My soul has been made over more beautiful and more radiant than ever before. I am the sum of God's divine wisdom, love, grace, compassion, beauty, depth, ingenuity, creativity, and kindness. The Creator, the Most High, bestowed all that upon me, instilled it in me.

How can I not win? How can I not have everything I want? Material is okay. But joy and peace. That's what I came here to get, that priceless joy and peace. I got it. This trip to the mountains was my own invitation to breathe. Inhale joy. And exhale peace.

Pablo Picasso, renowned as one of the greatest artists of the twentieth century, said, "Nothing can be accomplished without solitude." When you study the lives of great leaders, great inventors, great philanthropists, great writers, and great composers and philosophers, you find that solitude is a recurring theme. Their purpose was no greater than yours, and you too must embrace the silence. Turn off the radio when you're driving the car. Get up before the rest of your family and spend some time alone. Turn off the television, close your laptop, and silence your phone. Don't run from the thoughts and feelings that arise. Be still and sit with them. Ask God to show you what your purpose is or what the next step is in fulfilling it. You can use a practice of prayer or meditation, simply sit in a quiet place without distraction, or go for a hike that lets you enjoy the kind of silence you only find in nature. In your silence, don't just speak to Spirit, asking for what you want. Speak, ask, and then listen. God is always answering.

You were created on purpose and with a purpose. Trust yourself to hear the voice of God, who is always speaking to us and waiting for us to hear. Trust yourself to know your purpose when you see it. Trust yourself to take this journey even when it feels like you have to take it alone. God is always there, whispering to your spirit. All you have to do is listen and move accordingly.

Affirmation

I AM WALKING IN
MY DIVINE ASSIGNMENT.

THE JOURNEY BEYOND
BEGINS WITHIN

T HE ANCIENT ART OF RAINMAKING has been a spiritual practice around the world for centuries. On six of the seven continents on this planet, millions of people have believed in the power of creating or holding off rain for seasons, weddings, and outdoor events. In many African cultures, rainmaking represented the sacred relationship between humans and the Divine. Viewed as an extraordinary gift and the most explicit expression of God's goodness and love, rain, many believe, falls when the ancestors and gods are pleased. They don't consider it unusual to communicate with the cosmic force of God and command the elements; it's natural.

Along with chanting, praying, and fasting, shamans who pray for rain are often highly skilled and educated in weather patterns and environmental elements. They have worked for years to hone their abilities and show great courage in their calling. In other words, to see rain, rainmakers have to become diligent in their pursuit to make it rain. The Universe is not a respecter of fake words or temporary self-doubt. It hears what you say and responds accordingly. If you speak negatively of yourself and others, surely buckets of negativity will rain down in your life. The same is true when you speak kindly to yourself and about others. Then, gentle rain comes down in your life. You are your ultimate weatherman.

What if you train yourself just as the shamans have? By becoming skilled in the weather patterns and environmental elements in your life, you will begin to notice how your body, mind, and circumstances transform. As artist and spiritual teacher Florence Scovill Shinn said about your word, "It is your magic wand, for your word is God in action."[11] You will start to use your words like a wand, to create what you desire. John 1:1 (KJV) says, "In the beginning was the word, and the word was with God, and the word was God." Our words control our destiny and ultimately, our future. If you want to have loving relationships, a healthy marriage, financial freedom to bless yourself and others, or a healthy body, you have to speak it daily.

As you set out to create your breakthrough, I task you with only speaking the things you want to see, and none of what you don't. Watch the weather patterns and check your surroundings. I guarantee you will begin to see all the miracles of rain unfold right before your eyes. Thank God for the rain. Thank God for your ability to make it rain through your connection with the Divine. Thank God for the breakthrough that's already yours.

As Dr. Dennis Kimbro says in his book *What Makes the Great Great*, "If you are to have a new future, you need a new beginning."[12] Just as a baptism is meant to serve as a rebirth and a cleansing, this book is just that. You now get to define life on your own terms because you now understand that the power has been within you all along. In the prologue of the twenty-fifth-anniversary edition of *Discover the Power Within You*, Eric Butterworth illustrates this through the retelling of an old Hindu story of the gods and human divinity.[13] According to the legend, there was once a time when all humans were gods, but we abused our power.

Seeing this, Brahma, the chief god, called the council of gods together to discuss how they should go about hiding the divine power from human beings. They thought long and hard. One god suggested they hide the divine power deep in the Earth. Brahma immediately said no, for surely people would learn how to dig to the deepest parts of the Earth to reclaim their divine power. Another suggested they hide our divine power in the deepest parts of the ocean. Brahma said no, for surely, people would learn to dive to the deepest parts of the ocean to find their power. Brahma thought long and hard. Finally, he said, "We will hide their power deep within them; for surely, they will never seek to look within themselves to find their power."

Since the beginning of time, humans have been digging, diving, and climbing, trying to find that which is already within them. You should be tired of exerting energy on outside things when the real power to achieve greatness in your life lies within you. There is no magic pill and you cannot one-click it to your door by tomorrow. You have to do the work. There is a saying: "Just because you have the calculator doesn't mean you have the right answer." You have to show your work. Just like you did back in the day when you took your math test. You will need to show all of your work. Romans 12:2 (KJV) says, "And be not conformed to this world: but be ye transformed by the renewing of your mind, that ye may prove what is that good, and acceptable, and perfect will of God." In other words, the proof will be in the pudding. When you are transformed by the renewing of your mind, you will produce that which is good.

You will have to walk head first into your destiny. Elevate your circle and welcome new people into your life. Your friends should dare you to get out of the boat because they have decided to walk on water themselves. The people you spend the majority of your time with should inspire you to level up, not because they stand by cheering for you, but because they are aiming higher and hitting stars. You are now in the game of life. No more sitting on the sidelines and being a spectator in your own game. The choice for a better life is all yours. How you eat, think, speak, set boundaries in your life, and show up for yourself are all now a conscious choice. Life is not just happening to you; you are the conductor for wherever this train is going. Steer it in the direction of your destiny.

Don't waste another minute of your time. You will look back at this moment next year, two years, five years, and ten years from now and realize that success is so much easier than failing. Failing without growing is exhausting. You appreciate the lessons you've learned, but you're ready to pass go and move on to the next level in this game of life. Otherwise, failing makes us fearful and resentful. Our blessings don't grow in fearful, resentful, and unloving conditions, because God is not any of those things. You have the power within you to shift any atmosphere, perform miracles, and heal your life, because God is within you. Imagine what will happen when you resurrect the dreams and aspirations you let die. It will be as if you raised the dead, a true miracle.

You have received an invitation to your breakthrough. You have all you need to walk on water. Most importantly, you are not alone. God is with you and within you. I'm here to serve as a resource and guide for you along your journey, but the real work begins and ends with you. It's time to move in the direction of your highest good. You must accept and believe that God is an ever-present power within you. Let the Creator have its way. Let God show up in your life and the way you live it. My prayer for you, as you journey forward, is that you accept the divine power inside you. Loving God means loving yourself. Go get your breakthrough.

Affirmation

I AM GOD REVEALED ON EARTH.
I GIVE MYSELF PERMISSION
TO WALK ON WATER.

ENDNOTES

1   "The Big Move: Part 1." 1976. *Good Times.* Los
    Angeles, CA: CBS.

2   "The Big Move: Part 2." 1976. *Good Times.* Los
    Angeles, CA: CBS.

3   Truth, Sojourner. 2019. August 18. https://sourcebooks.
    fordham.edu/mod/sojtruth-woman.asp.

4   Houston, Pam. 2003. "The Truest Eye." Oprah.com.
    Harpo, Inc. Accessed August 18, 2019. http://www.oprah.
    com/omagazine/toni-morrison-talks-love/.

5   2019. "Lactose Intolerance - Genetics Home Reference
    - NIH." U.S. National Library of Medicine. National
    Institutes of Health. August 6, 2019. https://ghr.nlm.nih.
    gov/condition/lactose-intolerance.

6   2018. "Adult Obesity Facts | Overweight & Obesity |
    CDC." Centers for Disease Control and Prevention.
    Centers for Disease Control and Prevention. Accessed
    August 2019. https://www.cdc.gov/obesity/data/adult.html.

7   "FastStats - Health of Black or African American
    Population." Centers for Disease Control and Prevention.
    Centers for Disease Control and Prevention, 2017. https://
    www.cdc.gov/nchs/fastats/black-health.htm.

8   "Michael Bernard Beckwith." 2016. *Super Soul
    Sunday*. OWN.

9   Munroe, Myles. 1990. "The Power of Purpose." *Azusa
    Conference*. Accessed August 2019. https://www.youtube.
    com/watch?v=5iJyq-N_HZA.

10 Roosevelt, Theodore.1910. Accessed August 18,
    2019. theodorerooseveltcenter.org/Learn-About-TR/
    TR-Encyclopedia/Culture-and-Society/
    Man-in-the-Arena.aspx.

11 Scovill Shinn, Florence. *Your Word Is Your Wand*.
    Camarillo, California: DeVorss & Company, 1928.

12 Kimbro, Dennis Paul. *What Makes the Great Great:
    Strategies for Extraordinary Achievement*. New York:
    Broadway Books, 2003.

13 Butterworth, Eric. *Discover the Power within You: A
    Guide to the Unexplored Depths Within*. New York:
    HarperOne, 2008.

ACKNOWLEDGEMENTS

Candice Davis, you are a gift to the world. Thank you for your guidance and loving patience during the writing of this book. You helped me tell a beautiful story.

Karli Maya Raymond, thank you for supporting me through every rise and fall in my life. It is a joy to be your sister and friend. May our love and laugher bind us together forever. From the womb to the tomb. I love you.

Dr. Joy Beckwith Bakari. Thank you for helping me dig up the roots of my life and uncover all of its beauty. You have served as a wonderful teacher and guide on my journey to wellness. Wednesdays will forever be holy and sacred.

Keundric "Dooley" Loucious and my Effect Fitness Family. The turf has been the ultimate teacher. Thank you for helping me find a way to become better physically and mentally every single day.

To my Uncle Christopher Walter. Thank you for the years of standing in the gaps in my life, and for every time you asked how the book was coming along. You held me accountable. You will forever be one of my closest friends and confidants.

To my Grandmother Doris Walter, thank you for being that 10-year old girl in Louisville, Kentucky dressed in white and ready for baptism. You set us all on a path that day to find our own healing waters. Your prayers have and will always prevail.

To my Brothers Broderick and Wynton. I am blessed to have beautiful men like you in my life. I am grateful I get to bear witness to your unfolding. Let love be your guide.

To Oliver Muhammad. Thank you for all of our meetings on the moon. My heart will always echo your symphony.

To all the faithful subscribers of Beyond Her. Thank you for taking the journey BEYOND with me each week. May you be happy. May you be safe. May you be at ease. May you be at peace.

3/7/200

PArkoø 3/7/202

82 5

CPSIA information can be obtained
at www.ICGtesting.com
Printed in the USA
LVHW041322251119
638367LV00006B/42/P

9 781734 055207